THE STORY OF
BILLERICAY

THE STORY OF
BILLERICAY
CHARLES PHILLIPS

The
History
Press

First published 2013

The History Press
The Mill, Brimscombe Port
Stroud, Gloucestershire, GL5 2QG
www.thehistorypress.co.uk

British Library Cataloguing in Publication Data.
A catalogue record for this book is available from the British Library.

ISBN 978 0 7524 9924 6

Typesetting and origination by The History Press
Printed in Great Britain

CONTENTS

ACKNOWLEDGEMENTS

I wish to thank the following people and organisations:

Christine Brewster and the staff of the Cater Museum, Adrian Rilstone for writing the foreword, Father Jim McGrath, parish priest of Holy Redeemer, for his hospitality and help when I turned up unannounced at his presbytery front door, Billericay Musical Theatre Group, Barleylands Farm Museum, Julia Seaman, Sylvia Kent, Lord Petre for granting permission to reproduce the picture of his ancestor Sir William Petre, and for confirming information on Sir William and Sir John, later the First Baron Petre of Writtle, Malcolm Acors for guidance, Basildon Heritage for help with photographs, Denise Rowling, Jo Cullen, Susan Randle, the staff of Billericay Library who had to put up with me when I was doing my research, the staff of Chelmsford Library, the staff of Stock Library, the staff of Colchester Library, National Express East Anglia, the staff of Billericay station, Greater Anglia, the National Archive – formerly the Public Records Office, Essex Record Office, Jenny Butler, Stock Post Office and General Stores, the Great Eastern Railway Society, John Watling, Essex Bus Enthusiasts Group, Richard Delahoy, Essex County Council, Billericay Town Council, Ken Butcher, Alan Osborne, Simon Fletcher, the late David Collins, Billericay History, Jim Devlin, Roger Watling, the British Newspaper Library, Trove – Australian On Line Newspaper Archive, National Library of New Zealand Newspaper Archive, Project Gutenburg and British History Online.

FOREWORD

I t would be discourteous of me not to begin by admitting that I feel flattered and privileged to have been asked to write this foreword for Charles Phillips's *The Story of Billericay*. I can only claim to be a native by adoption, but by way of mitigation I was very young when brought, with my sister, to Billericay by my father and mother, and I certainly remember the town as it must have been – with, of course, change of personnel although not necessarily of family – for many generations before our arrival in 1950.

Charles outlines the development of the town from the Stone Age, through its over-powering annexing of Great Burstead to the present day. He is, as I know from personal experience, passionate about a similar over-powering annexing of Billericay by Basildon, and ends his book with what can only be read as a clarion call to Billericay residents to search out a twenty-first-century Wat Tyler!

I happily commend this volume to all, and am sure that it will be as important to Billericay and Essex bibliophiles as its many predecessors referred to in Charles's list of sources.

Adrian Rilstone, 2009

INTRODUCTION

Billericay's history goes back a very long way, and unlike a lot of towns it still has a good number of its historic buildings and other reminders of the past. For the purposes of this book I have focused on the area known as Billericay today. Historically it was part of the parish of Great Burstead, so I have included information about that area too: it is often impossible to unravel references to the two settlements in the sources.

I was born in St Andrew's Hospital in Billericay, and for many years used Billericay station when travelling to work in London. Following early retirement in 2005 I have seen more of the town than when I was working, and have felt for some time that there is a need for a new written history. This is not to decry the work of those who have gone before me. In researching I have been fortunate in having access to a number of sources that were not easily available to earlier historians. This is primarily thanks to the wonders of the internet – and all those people who are taking the time to make sometimes obscure material available to the wider world.

This book is dedicated to the people of Billericay. While taking photographs and undertaking research for this book I walked and cycled around large parts of Billericay and Great Burstead. It was an education – and I hope you learn as much from reading this book as I did from writing it.

I fully accept that through no fault of my own errors may well have occurred or been perpetuated. I whole heartedly apologise if that has happened. If you have any comments please contact me via the email address below or via the publishers.

Charles Phillips
Stock, near Billericay
October 2012
charlesetphillips@yahoo.co.uk

one

STONE AGE TO SAXONS

I t is not known when the first people settled in the area that is now Billericay, but evidence has been found of Middle Stone Age activity in the shape of some burnt bone, pottery and a flint axe head on the south-east-facing slope less than a mile from the town. Beyond this, which suggests a settlement of some kind, not a great deal is known about Billericay in the Middle Stone Age.

There was definitely a settlement here by the time of the Bronze Age. Two Bronze Age burial mounds were excavated in Norsey Wood from 1865 onwards. Finds included burials and Deverel-Rimbury pottery, dating from 2500 to 1000 BC. This distinctive pottery is in the most characteristic Middle Bronze Age style – globular thick-walled urns, with smooth surfaces and subtle decoration. The number of dead found in these burial mounds indicates that they were used over a long period of time, which suggests a settlement of some importance. Its exact location in relation to the modern town cannot now be determined, as the timber Bronze Age huts, probably with turf roofs, have left no trace. While the burial mound in the south-eastern part of Norsey Wood is a Scheduled Ancient Monument, the one near the Norsey Road has had an air-raid shelter, a fish pond and a garage (among other things) built into it at various times since the 1930s.

The arrival of the Iron Age, which ran roughly from 500 BC to the coming of the Romans, brought with it more concrete evidence of a settlement. In pre-Roman times Essex was inhabited by the powerful Trinovantes tribe, whose territory covered an area at least from modern Colchester to the mouth of the Thames. Downham Grange near Billericay is thought to have been an Iron Age fort to protect the area from the south-west, north-east and east. This survived the Roman occupation and was used thereafter by the Saxons. Unfortunately no remains can be found today. From limited evidence, it has been suggested that Iron Age Billericay consisted of about a dozen families living in farmsteads

The Bronze Age barrow in Norsey Wood is the oldest surviving structure in Billericay. (Author)

that contained three generations; this led to a tribal organisation. The buildings were large, thatched and circular, made of wattle and daub, and with an opening in the roof for smoke to escape. Wattle and daub construction consisted of interwoven twigs plastered with a mixture of clay, lime, water, and sometimes dung and chopped straw.

Relics from the Iron Age have been found over the years, particularly on the high ground behind the former St Andrew's Hospital. When the cutting for the railway was being dug in the mid-1880s an Iron Age burial urn was found. At Bell Hill in the mid-1970s, during the building of a new housing development, a ditch or stream bed produced Iron Age material and evidence of an area of extensive burning, which possibly dated from the Iron Age. Archaeologists recorded a ditch that produced stratified material from the first century AD, but it is not certain if this was Iron Age or Roman. At some unknown date an Iron Age pot was found in the garden of 5 Chapel Street.

The Romans briefly invaded Britain in 55 BC and 54 BC under Julius Caesar. These invasions were not successful from the Roman point of view, however, and it was AD 43 before they came again. This was the start of the Roman occupation of Britain. They established a military station of the Ninth Legion in Norsey Wood. The headquarters of the Ninth Legion was built at Colchester. Although this was destroyed in the revolt of AD 61 led by Queen Boudicca, it was later rebuilt.

There is definitive evidence of a large Roman settlement in Billericay, although its Roman name is not known, and many vestiges of the period have been found in the town. These include coins, bricks, pottery, brooches and numerous other artefacts, and at Sun Corner the remains of Roman buildings have been found. In 1877, during the digging of a hole for the building of a gasometer at the gasworks in Laindon Road, workmen came across a cache of broken pottery on a platform or pavement of Roman construction. This pottery, on investigation by Mr J.A. Sparvel-Bayley, was found to be cinerary (that is, it contained the ashes of the dead), and other urns including some of Samian ware, one of which bore the word DACMUS. In 1933 part of a Roman rubbish pit was excavated in Norsey Wood. This revealed late fourth-century coins and pottery. The concurrent discovery of late Iron Age pottery was clear evidence that this rubbish pit had been in use for centuries. Excavations in 1987–8 at School Road and Roman Way revealed cremation burials, wells and ditches of the first to fourth centuries AD. A pottery kiln dated AD 43 to 100 was discovered to the south of the school in Buckenhams Field just north of the junction of Laindon and Noak Hill roads.

The Roman settlement stretched in an arc from near the site of St Mary Magdalen's Church in the High Street to Norsey Wood. This position provided a defensive view over surrounding forests. Some sources think that during the Roman occupation an additional outpost, possibly a fort, was built at Blunts Wall, near Tye Common and west of the High Street. From the evidence that has been found of a Roman road that went from Norsey Wood to Stock, it seems that the main road through Roman Billericay ran from the Roman settlement at Chelmsford (Caesaromagus) to the Thames. Other evidence of a Roman road was found during building work at Billericay School.

Bell Hill and the drovers' pond. (Basildon Heritage)

It is worth remembering that the Roman occupation of Britain was just that: an occupation. Although it lasted from AD 43 to 410 and there were Roman buildings and Roman towns throughout much of Britain, there was not the same assimilation that occurred in France or Spain. Billericay at this time, for example, consisted of a Roman occupation force existing side by side with the indigenous population. Roman law and a few other habits of life were imposed on the inhabitants, but they were essentially free to go about their own business. There is evidence that some in the higher echelons of society adopted a Roman way of life, living in Roman-style buildings but remaining essentially British; Romano-British. Humbler folk remained British even in the style of their buildings, but no doubt some of their number understood and were able to read and write a modicum of Latin. Co-operation and collaboration took place. It is possible that there were liaisons between the occupying forces and local inhabitants, and that some male inhabitants joined the Roman army as auxiliaries, that is non-citizen corps.

By the end of the fourth century AD the Roman Empire was coming under attack along its fringes, including Britain, and in 383 the Roman army began to withdraw from its British territory. This withdrawal was completed in 410. Essex was eventually settled by Saxons from Lower Saxony, in what is now Germany. Records from the period are scarce, so we do not know how long their conquest of the area took. From the evidence of a wheel-turned pot of Roman ware found at Billericay, there is a suggestion that the Saxon conquest might have taken place over a long period, commencing some time before the withdrawal of the Romans. The pot, which contained human ashes, indicates that there was a gradual intermingling of Saxon and Roman cultures: it has Saxon decoration (a cruciform pattern, lines and dots and a swastika) and a fourth-century Roman jar as its lid.

Eventually Roman Billericay was deserted. The reason for this was that the Saxons associated cemeteries with ghosts, and in the Roman settlement there were cemeteries. The Saxon invaders settled at a new site, now Great Burstead. This had an impact on Billericay which lasted for centuries: it was not until 1844 that Billericay was finally separated from Great Burstead, and became a separate ecclesiastical parish.

Norsey Wood is where Billericay began, but what of the place itself? It is a mixed coppiced woodland of 165 acres, varying in height from 197ft to 302ft above sea level. The wood comprises plateaus of sandy soils overlying clays, producing four valleys that lead into a principal valley. The steep-sided but well-vegetated valleys radiate in a northward direction from the south-west corner of the wood, and during the winter and wet periods contain southward flowing streams. These eventually lead into the River Crouch. The higher plateau areas are reasonably flat and well drained and gently slope northwards. In the north-east the gravels become thinner, and the underlying clays support small springs, although with today's warmer climate these have largely become redundant. For such reasons there exist three apparently artificial ponds in the north-east of the wood, and one in the south-east. The gravel plateaus mainly support sweet chestnut coppice, and in the south and east areas of hornbeam, oak, birch, rowan and aspen. The marshy valleys support alder, ash and willow coppice with areas of pendulous sedge, sphagnum moss and buckler fern. The soils in Norsey Wood are very acidic.

There is a well-defined system of 'rides' in the wood. The primary one is believed to date back to Iron Age times, if not to the Bronze Age. By the end of the sixteenth century the major rides were sufficiently established to appear on a map of the area; this dates from 1593. In more recent years a series of footpaths has developed.

The main historical features that are easily visible are the Bronze Age burial mound, medieval deerbanks (protective boundaries consisting of a massive ditch and bank, a formidable barrier for animals) and First and Second World War trenches.

Before the early 1930s the area of the wood was about 200 acres. It included within its boundaries a second Bronze Age burial mound. However, housing development in 1931 to 1933 reduced the wood to its present size – and, as mentioned elsewhere, a house was built on the other Bronze Age burial mound. This housing development also destroyed a large part of the northern section of the medieval deerbanks.

The whole of Norsey Wood is a Scheduled Ancient Monument, and it is also a local nature reserve.

The medieval deerbank in Norsey Wood. (Author)

two

THE NORMAN CONQUEST AND
THE MEDIEVAL TOWN

I n 1066 William, Duke of Normandy (William the Conqueror) successfully invaded England. As King William I he commissioned a survey
in 1085 of all the land that he had acquired. This was known as the
Domesday Book, and was compiled between 1086 and 1087 by commissioners who travelled around the country, which was divided into seven
circuits. It was not a population census but a land and property census: King
William wanted to know who held what land, the number of working persons
there were, what animals there were and what money he could expect to receive
from the land. Although it contains a wealth of information, the Domesday
Book omits certain places: there are no records specifically relating to the City
of London, for example. It also mentions only working people: no attempt is
made to record their spouses or children.

As far as is known Billericay does not appear in the Domesday Book. It
was suggested by the Rev. George Walker in his book *The Story of a Little Town*
(1947) that the reference in Domesday to land held by the Bishop of Bayeux
in Great and Little Burstead acquired since the Conquest relates to Billericay.
This land had twenty-eight freemen holding 28 hides (a hide was notionally the
amount of land that would support a household) and 5 acres (medieval acres
were different from modern acres; they could be used to measure length as
well as area). At the time of the Conquest there were sixteen ploughlands, but
at the time of the survey thirteen. A ploughland was the amount of land that
could be ploughed in one year using a plough and a team of eight oxen. The
land had 5 hides of woodland, 23 acres of meadow, pasture for 250 sheep, 54
bordars (a type of peasant), and 4 slaves. It had decreased in value from £20 at
the time of the Conquest to £16 at the time of the survey.

For the sake of completeness I will give you details of the rest of the land held
by the Bishop of Bayeux in Great and Little Burstead. Before the Conquest
the land was held as one manor by Ingvar, who was a thane – part of the king's

18

Hundred of BARSTABLE

1 Thorold's son holds VANGE from the Bishop. 2 free men held it
for 5½ hides. Always 2 ploughs in lordship; 4 men's ploughs.
6 villagers; 9 smallholders; 1 slave.
Woodland, ½ hide; pasture, 120 sheep; 1 fishery; now 1 mill.
2 cobs, 4 cattle, 4 pigs; then 67 sheep, now 270.
Of this land, 1 free man held 30 acres which were added to the
aforesaid land after 1066; it is not known how.
Value then 100s; now £8.

2 The Bishop holds (Great) BURSTEAD in lordship. Ingvar, a thane,
held it before 1066 as 1 manor, 10 hides. Always 3 ploughs in
lordship. Then 12 men's ploughs, now 11.
Then 20 villagers, now 22; then 5 smallholders, now 10.
Woodland, ½ hide; pasture, 150 sheep. 2 cobs, 11 cattle,
106 pigs, 219 sheep.
Value £20.
28 free men were added to this manor after 1066; they hold
28 hides and 5 acres. On these there were then 16 ploughs, now 13.
Woodland, 5 hides; meadow, 23 acres; pasture, 250 sheep.
54 smallholders, 4 slaves.
Value of this addition then £20; now [£] 16.

3 The Bishop holds DUNTON in lordship. 1 priest, a free man, held it
before 1066 for 7 hides and 40 acres. Then 4 ploughs in lordship,
now 2. Always 4 men's ploughs.
Then 7 villagers, now 2; 6 smallholders; then 5 slaves, now 2.
2 cobs, 2 cattle, 15 pigs, 34 sheep.
Value then £12; now [£] 7.

4 Thorold's son holds BARSTABLE (Hall) from the Bishop. 1 free
man held it for 5½ hides and 30 acres.
Woodland, 30 acres; pasture, 100 sheep.
Always 3 ploughs in lordship; 2 men's [ploughs].
6 villagers, 11 smallholders.
Value then £4; now 100s.
In lordship then 2 cobs, 5 cattle, 18 pigs, 36 sheep; now 1 cob,
9 cattle, 24 pigs, 80 sheep.

Great Burstead in the Domesday Book.
(Phillimore)

or a lord's household, or part of a military elite. The land area was 10 hides. Of this land three ploughlands always belonged to the lordship of the manor. Obviously there had been some reduction in land available for ploughing, as before the Conquest the men held twelve ploughlands but at the time of Domesday they only had eleven. At the time of the Conquest there were twenty villagers and five smallholders; at Domesday there were twenty-two villagers and ten smallholders. A villager was a member of the peasant class who held the most land; a smallholder was a 'middle-class' peasant. There was half a hide of woodland and also pasture. The Domesday Book says that there were 150 sheep, 2 cobs, 11 cattle, 106 pigs and 219 sheep; this second reference to sheep is confusing. The land was valued at £20. It may be noted that the area of newly acquired land at Great Burstead was greater than the area called Great Burstead at the time of the Conquest.

At the time of Domesday the Bishop of Bayeux was one Odo, the half-brother of William the Conqueror. In 1082 he was imprisoned for seditious behaviour, and in 1088 raised a rebellion against his nephew William Rufus. The rebellion failed, and Odo was banished from the country. Because of his disgrace the manor of Great Burstead passed to the Marshall family, whose head was the Earl of Pembroke under the second creation of the title in 1189.

William Marshall, Earl of Pembroke granted it to Richard Siward, who then granted it to Stratford Langthorne Abbey at Bow. The monks of the abbey were Cistercians.

The first Essex historian, the Rev. Philip Morant (1700–70), says in his *History and Antiquities of the County of Essex* (1760–8) that 'Billericay is a hamlet in Great Burstead, but so considerable as to be a market town; the only one within this hundred [Barstable Hundred] except the little town of Horndon on the Hill.' Another name for Great Burstead was Burstead Grange – a grange being a monastic estate used for food production, or sometimes the agricultural buildings at the heart of that estate. The Cistercians had been discharged by Popes Paschal II and Hadrian IV of paying tithes on land they tilled themselves, and so in general they did not let out their lands, thereby making themselves liable for the paying of tithes, and had large barns or granges in which to store their crops.

As to when this 'hamlet' of Billericay was first established … we don't know. We can make an educated guess as to why it was established, though: a settlement appears to have grown up where the road from Chelmsford to the Thames joined the road from London to Wickford on the River Crouch, which in those days is believed to have been navigable as far as Wickford. Today's Chelmsford, however, can only be traced back to about 1100, when Maurice, Bishop of London built a bridge across the River Cam. This theory apparently contradicts George Walker's suggestion that the extra land held by the time of Domesday was the settlement now known as Billericay. Exactly when and why the hamlet was established remains shrouded in mystery.

According to Philip Morant, the first time Billericay is mentioned is in 1343, when Thomas Malegreff is recorded to have held of Humphrey de Bohun, the 6th Earl of Hereford under the sixth creation and the 5th Earl of Essex under the third creation, the hamlet of Beleuca in Burstead as of his manor of Fobbying (Fobbing). Morant says that this name Beleuca is probably derived from the old word Baleuga or Banleuga, denoting territory or precinct round a borough or manor; the French word banlieue, suburb, is from the same root. He says that by 1395 Beleuca had been transformed into Billerica, but he does not know how this transformation came about.

According to Percy Hide Reaney in his *Place Names of Essex* (1935), however, the earliest mention of Billericay is in 1291, when it was spelt Byllyrica. By 1307 the spelling has changed to Billirica; in 1343 it is Billerica. This contradicts Morant's findings. How to explain the two contradictory names for Billericay in 1343? Perhaps Billerica refers to the hamlet and Beleuca to the territory or precinct around it.

While a large part of Billericay was located in Great Burstead, there was a small part of it that was in Mountnessing in the manor of Cowbridge, which according to Morant extended along the High Street as far as the Red Lion. At the time of the Conquest Cowbridge was owned by one Alwin, but when the Domesday Book was compiled it was owned by one Ranulf, brother of Ilger, who was a minister of the crown. Later the manor gave its name to a family, and we find Richard de Cobridge mentioned in a deed of Roger de Ginges in the reign of Henry III. Next, the manor became part of the possessions of Stratford Langthorne Abbey.

According to Harry Richman in *Billericay and its High Street* (second edition, 1965) in about 1342 a chantry chapel was established in Billericay. This date slightly contradicts Philip Morant. A chantry was a private Mass celebrated regularly for the repose of the soul of a testator and others nominated by them in their will. Some were endowed during the lifetime of the founder, and the Mass priest was obliged to celebrate Masses for his well-being while he was alive and his soul after death. Chantries were also endowed by guilds and fraternities for the benefit of their members, and even the most humble testator could arrange for one or two Masses to be said for his soul. Those who had the most money were responsible for the erection of magnificent chantry chapels. However, history is never straightforward and there is some confusion about the establishment of Billericay's chantry chapel, which eventually became the church of St Mary Magdalen. Harry Richman says that, 'It is usually stated that about 1342 a chapel and chantry with lands to support a priest was founded in Billericay by a member of the Sulyard family of Flemyng's, Runwell', but there seems to be a slight mystery here judging by Morant's account. He states that the Sulyards were only at Flemyng's (now Flemings) from the late fifteenth century: John Flemyng inherited from his father in 1464, aged fifteen, then died without issue leaving three sisters; at this point the Sulyards come into the story. All this means that the Billericay chapel and chantry were founded long before the Sulyards were at Flemyngs, if 1342 is the right date. However, J.A. Sparvel-Bayley, writing in the *Essex Archaeological Transaction* at the end of the nineteenth century, stated that it had not been satisfactorily ascertained when the chapel was founded. He said that Newcourt in his Repertorium attributed the foundation of the chapel to the Sulyards family, of Flemmings in Runwell.

In 1367 the Chantry House in the High Street was built, and according to a report in the *Daily Chronicle* in June 1926 (at the time of its proposed sale and removal to America) it was renovated in 1510. According to the article, the building was at one time 'used as a meeting place for priests, who said their masses in the private chapel' in the house.

Morant also says that because of flooding during the winter, when the inhabitants of the western part of Billericay could not easily reach their parish church of 'Ging Mountney' (Mountnessing), the vicar of Great Burstead was to 'receive the small tithes and oblations of Blunts Wall', which was one of the manors of Great Burstead. He concludes that 'we will suppose this chapel built as well for the chantry, as for the ease of these inhabitants now laid to Billericay'. Perhaps residents contributed to the purchase of the chantry lands, or paid for the priest through voluntary contributions: 'it is plain a priest was maintained and according to the Book of Chantries, did sing mass and minister sacraments, which last was not the office of a mere chantry priest'.

The original name of the chapel, which later became the parish church, was not St Mary Magdalen (as it became later) but St John the Baptist.

There was also a primitive fort at Blunts Wall during this period. As mentioned in the previous chapter, some sources think that there was a fort on this site in Roman times. While the new fort dated from the thirteenth century, it would have made sense to make use of the remains of an earlier fort in its construction. Until comparatively recently some earthworks survived: the remains of a ditch and ramparts, together with some artificial mounds. They have now been obliterated.

In 1253 there is reference made to a market in Great Burstead. On 14 May of that year Henry III granted the Abbey of Stratford Langthorne the licence to hold a market at Great Burstead on a Tuesday and a fair there on the vigil, the day and morrow of the feast of St Mary Magdalen. In 1285 Edward I confirmed the earlier charter. It is not known where the market was held, whether it was in Great Burstead itself or in what is now Billericay.

During the twelfth and thirteenth centuries Norsey Wood was part of the Forest of Essex, which was Royal Forest – the king's hunting ground, protected by Forest Law. Under this legislation landowners could only hunt or take wood out of the forest with the king's permission, and the granting of a licence. To create permanent boundaries in order to prevent deer and cattle entering the wood, landowners built huge ditch and bank systems around their woods; as previously mentioned, Norsey Wood's bank was named the Deerbank –

St Mary Magdalen church, *c*.1900. (Basildon Heritage)

High Street and Chantry House, 1900s. (Basildon Heritage)

a unique title. The bank that survives today is of a later construction than the original one, upon which it was superimposed.

A very important event in the fourteenth century that the men of Billericay took part in was the Peasants' Revolt of 1381. The reasons for this uprising included excessive taxation, the extravagance of the royal court, the imposition of dues by the lords of the manors and the failure of the English government to protect English homes from French and Spanish naval attack. There was also the matter of a poll tax that had been imposed by the government in November 1380 to raise money for the war against France then in progress. This was a tax of 3 groats on everyone over fifteen, except paupers; a groat was worth four old pennies. Naturally, because the new poll tax took a larger proportion of the income of the poor than it did of the rich, it was not popular. J.A. Sparvel-Bayley, writing in the *Essex Archaeological Transactions*, says that 'the tax ... was rigorously exacted, the insolence of its collectors being but too often unbounded; opposition was everywhere offered, and in no county more so than in Essex, and especially by the men of Fobbing, Stanford [le Hope], Billericay and Hadleigh'. The Revolt started on 30 May 1381, when the villagers of Fobbing, Corringham and Stanford-le-Hope as well as others from Stock, Ingatestone, Warley and Ramsden (Bellhouse), and a weaver dwelling in Billericay, attacked the King's Commissioner of Taxes and John Bampton, an Essex JP, when the commissioner went to Brentwood to reassess the return for the Barstable Hundred. The absolute refusal of the men of Fobbing to co-operate led to an outbreak of violence when John Bampton foolishly ordered the king's sergeants at arms to arrest the men's spokesman. The commissioner and his men, who were lucky to escape with their lives, fled to London to report the incident to the government. Undeterred, and still in ignorance of the true situation, the authorities made further attempts to enforce the tax and apprehend those involved in the riot. The Chief Justice of the Common Pleas, Sir Robert Belknap, was commissioned to bring them to justice. However, on 2 June at Brentwood he and his retinue were also attacked by the still recalcitrant villagers; the court was wrecked and its papers destroyed. The fracas developed to the point of murderous violence, and the rioters beheaded three local jurors. After this the situation deteriorated even further, and serious disorder spread throughout Essex.

Rioting also occurred in Kent. Tradition has it that the reason for this outbreak was a gross act of violence by one of the tax collectors against the young daughter of a tradesman living in Dartford. In retaliation, he killed the tax collector – apparently by hitting his head with a hammer. When the news of what had happened in Kent reached Essex, the rebels there crossed the Thames and joined up with those of Kent.

Meanwhile the revolt spread further. Manor houses and religious houses were attacked, the houses of unpopular lords of the manor and justices were pillaged, and court rolls were burnt. The rebels invaded London and killed, among others, the Archbishop of Canterbury. The young king Richard II met them at Mile End and granted commutation of all dues for a rent of 4d per acre, and a free pardon for all rebels. This was written down, which satisfied most of the rebels, although those who refused to submit were summarily executed in the presence of the others. Shortly afterwards the king called out his soldiers and rode out to Waltham (Holy Cross) to punish the rebellion with cruel severity. The charters of liberation were repealed by Parliament as having been extorted under pressure.

This wasn't the end. After the rebels had dispersed from Waltham, full of anger and disappointment, those from Essex reassembled at Billericay, Rettendon and Great Baddow, where they prepared to continue their resistance. At Norsey Wood they assembled to make a last stand against the pursuing army of Sir Thomas Plantagent of Woodstock, the Earl of Buckingham and Sir Thomas de Percy. Although well prepared and great in number, the ignorant and poorly trained peasants were no match against the trained army. Over 500 were killed, and 800 of their horses were taken. Those who survived fled to Colchester, but failed to stir up trouble there. After that they went to Sudbury, in Suffolk, but Lord Fitzwalter and Sir John Harlestone pursued them, killed some and put the rest in prison.

During the nineteenth century a workman digging gravel in Norsey Wood described a ditch and a cave he discovered, which may been connected with the last stand of the Peasants' Revolt. In *The History of Norsey Wood* K.G. Cook quoted an unknown person, possibly the Rev. J.E.K. Cutts, as saying that 'one of the labourers informed me that in levelling and digging for gravel he came upon a ditch, about 8 feet deep, and wide enough for one person to walk along; it was about three hundred yards along, and at the end was a circular cave about the same depth as the ditch, and 15 feet in diameter; in it was some charcoal and several pieces of brick about two inches thick'.

After the revolt a number of properties were seized by the crown from those who had been outlawed or executed for taking part in the revolt. In some instances their descendants were able to claim it back, but not all were successful. In about 1401 Lors Brigg, the daughter of Roger Underwode, who was probably one of those hanged after the battle in Norsey Wood, was able to claim his property back from the crown. However, the property held by Thomas Ledre, who was executed after the revolt, was lost to the heirs and assigns of his widow Katherine, who had remarried.

From 1476 there is definite evidence of a market being held in Billericay. On 19 December of that year Edward IV granted to the monks of Stratford Langthorne Abbey a charter to hold a market at Billericay each Wednesday, as well as two annual fairs of three days each at the feasts of St Mary Magdalen and the Decollation (Beheading) of St John (the Baptist). Billericay men did not only attend their own market; they also went to others. For example, in 1491 it is recorded that Thomas Roos and William Prentys of Billericay were allowed exemption from market tolls at Colchester as they were tenants of the Duchy of Lancaster, whose special privileges included exemption from market tolls at such places as Colchester.

In the earlier mention of a weaver dwelling in Billericay who took part in the Peasants' Revolt we have the first evidence of a weaving industry in the town; this survived into the eighteenth century. While Billericay was a centre for weaving, it was only a minor one – unlike Colchester, Coggeshall, Braintree

Norsey Wood, the scene of the last stand of the Peasants' Revolt. (Author)

The Red Lion dates back to the fifteenth century and was the headquarters of the courts leet and baron under the Petre family, lords of the manor of Great Burstead. (Author)

and Bocking. Billericay was also a centre for wool export. Billericay woolmen collected wool from farmers at market or direct from farms in the area, and stored it in warehouses in the High Street until it was shipped overseas. The main destination for the wool was Flanders, one of the territories that constituted the Low Countries (now the Netherlands, Belgium and part of France). The wool was conveyed by packhorse either to the Crouch at Battlesbridge (or Wickford if navigation was possible as far as there) or the Thames at Grays, Benfleet or Leigh; and thence by ship to Flanders. Further evidence of the woollen industry in Billericay comes from the court rolls of the Corporation of Colchester and the records of Maldon's civil courts. In 1402, for example, the court rolls record that 'Benedict Wollemongere, John Stace, John Tannere, Thomas Blowere and Richard Markaunt of Billericay, buyers of wools, have several times come to the town market and carried off, each for himself, wool, mangy and watery, which they expose for sale to the burgesses as well as to foreigners to the great deception, and against the ordinances of the town, in mercy 12d each.' Apparently they bought bad wool and tried to pass it off as good. It seems likely that John Tannere was also involved in a case in Maldon's civil courts in 1423: it is recorded that John Tanner, a woolman of Billericay, sued John Friday, a weaver of Maldon.

Looking through the records of the Court of Common Pleas concerning market and trading privileges in the hinterland of medieval London for the period before the Reformation, we find that in April 1380 a pardon of outlawry was granted to William Parker of Burstead for non-appearance to render £20 10s to John Hervy of London. From circumstantial evidence it seems likely that William Parker came from Billericay. From the records of the same court we learn that in February 1402 a pardon of outlawry was granted to John Godegroom, a London butcher, for non-appearance to answer for a debt of 6 marks 4d to Roger Tannere of Billericay. Also from the records of the Court of Common Pleas for 1402, a case of a writ for debt involved property at Billericay. Richard Coksale, a saddler of London, claimed that on 10 August 1395 he 'demised' (leased) to John Bourer, a turner of London and his wife Alice, alias Alice Torold, a messuage (a house and the ground around it) and 34 acres of land with appurtenances (rights and obligations) in Billericay, for fifteen years and for an annual rent of 13s 4d, payable in equal portions at Easter and Michaelmas. The defendants had failed to pay the 5 marks 6s 8d in arrears and due on the day of the original writ of 8 March 1402, and he claimed damages of £20. Richard Coksale and the Bourers were back before the court in 1404 – again arguing about arrears.

BILLERICAY MEN NAMED IN THE PEASANTS' REVOLT

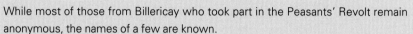

While most of those from Billericay who took part in the Peasants' Revolt remain anonymous, the names of a few are known.

The most famous person to take part is only known by his trade – the 'certain weaver from Billericay' who took part in the attack at Brentwood on 30 May 1381. He is mentioned in the inquisitions held at Chelmsford on Thursday 4 July: 'It was presented that numerous persons of Fobbyng, Stanford, Mokkyng and Horndon, with a certain weaver dwelling in Billericay …'

On 26 June 1381 one Thomas Plomer from Billericay was beheaded. From the evidence available it would seem that he was one of the rebels who were executed by the government.

In the Coram Rege Roll of 1381–2 we find two names. This roll records court proceedings that were supposed to be carried out before the king in person (*coram rege*), although this was rarely the case. Firstly there is a 'Precept to the Sheriff [of Essex] to search for numerous persons including Walter Cartere of Billerica, from county to county to summon them if not outlawed, or to take them if outlawed and to have their bodies before the King in the octaves of St Michael to answer to the King for divers felonies …' Secondly there is a 'Precept to the Sheriff to search for Roger Forster of Billerica, alias Roger Underwode of the same place … and to have his body before the King in the Octaves of Holy Trinity to answer to the King wherefore he broke the King's Marshalcy to which he had been committed for certain felonies whereof he had been indicted, and feloniously escaped from the same'.

three

THE REFORMATION

The Reformation was the most important event in English history in the sixteenth century. It was caused by the refusal in 1533 of Pope Julius II to annul the marriage of King Henry VIII to his wife of twenty-two years, Catherine of Aragon, because she had not borne him a male heir and so that he could marry Anne Boleyn. Catherine had previously been married to Henry's elder brother Arthur, who had died before ascending the throne. Henry's argument for wanting an annulment and the Pope's refusal for granting it were based on their interpretations of the Old Testament books of Leviticus and Deuteronomy. Deuteronomy said it was lawful for a man to marry his brother's widow; Leviticus said that it was not. To slightly complicate things, before Catherine married Henry a dispensation had had to be obtained from the Pope in order to overrule the impediment of affinity. She had had to swear that her marriage was unconsummated – which may or may not have been true. When the Pope did not give Henry the result he wanted he split with Rome, and in 1534 made himself head of the Church in England. Ironically, some years before this Henry had been very devout in his following of the Catholic faith in the face of the first stirrings of Protestantism, to such an extent that the Pope gave him the title 'Defender of the Faith'.

What happened in Billericay at the time of the Reformation in general terms is not clear, but it is likely that little changed: Catholicism was the order of the day, minus the Pope's authority and with the use of English in some parts of the services. Not everyone accepted this, some still regarding the Pope as the head of the Church. John Tyrel, who was influenced by new Protestant teachings, was burnt at the stake in Billericay for his beliefs – in 1527, before Henry's break with Rome.

The main event to affect Billericay initially was the Dissolution of the Monasteries. Henry VIII regarded them as the last vestiges of the Pope's power in England. Not all monasteries were dissolved at the same time, the whole

The exterior of St Mary Magdalen church. The original building of 1342 was rebuilt in 1490, and again during the eighteenth century. (Author)

The interior of St Mary Magdalen church. (Author, with thanks to Billericay and Little Burstead team ministry)

process taking from 1536 to 1540. The smaller establishments were lost first, and the largest last; Stratford Langthorne was not dissolved until 1538. An individual who benefited from the Dissolution was an Oxford lawyer, William Petre (c.1505–72), who originally came from Torbryan near Totnes in Devon and gained an introduction to Henry's court through the Boleyn family, being appointed a clerk in Chancery and later deputy to Thomas Cromwell, Henry's Chief Secretary and Vicar General for ecclesiastical affairs. Petre acted as visitor to the monastic houses in southern England and supervised, among much else, the dissolution of Barking Abbey in 1539. This was the greatest abbey in England at that time, its abbess ranking as a peeress of the realm. In 1537 Petre secured the lease of the manor of Great Burstead Grange from the Abbey of Stratford Langthorne, but he soon disposed of this and in the following year acquired the lease of the manor of Ingatestone, from Barking Abbey. In 1543 he was knighted by the king. Sir William Petre was an interesting man, who managed to keep the favour of whichever monarch was in power, whether of Protestant or Catholic persuasion – quite a feat at that time. During the reign of Protestant monarchs he was a secretly practising Catholic, a practice that was followed by his son John, later Sir John and later Baron Petre of Writtle. Later members of the family were quite openly Catholic.

In 1539 Great Burstead, which was now owned by the king, was leased to Sir Richard Riche. Sir Richard was a successful lawyer and politician, the founder of Felsted School, the MP for Colchester from 1529 to 1548 and, on elevation to the peerage as Lord Riche, Lord Chancellor from 1549 to 1551. On 30 October 1551 he obtained a licence to alienate (that is to transfer the ownership of) the manor, together with the rectory and advowson of the vicarage, to Thomas Marshe. It is likely that the sale did not go ahead, because when he died on 12 June 1566 he still possessed the premises, which were inherited by his second son and heir Robert Lord Riche, who gave it by his will when he died (on 25 February 1580) to his third son Sir Edwin Riche, who sold it on 2 September 1600 to Sir William Petre's son Sir John Petre; he was created Baron Petre of Writtle on 21 July 1603. The manor has remained in the family since.

The manor of Cowbridge also came into Sir Richard Riche's ownership after the Dissolution of the Monasteries, but on 4 March 1555 he transferred it to Sir William Petre for £453 10s.

Henry was also keen to abolish all free chapels, chantries and colleges, together with all hospitals, brotherhoods and guilds of a purely ecclesiastical

nature, and to vest their assets in himself. He attempted to do this through an Act of 1545, but before many of these important educational and charitable foundations had been dissolved Henry died, thus rendering the Act inoperative. It is not known how many of the establishments were lost.

Henry was succeeded on his death by his son Edward VI, the result of his third marriage to Jane Seymour. During Edward's reign the Reformation continued. Shrines were destroyed and in 1547 chantries were abolished. The commission that had been appointed in the king's name to report on the chantries of Essex described John Beforde, the priest in charge of

Sir William Petre. (Lord Petre)

the chantry chapel of Great Burstead (i.e. Billericay), as 'of small learning, very lame and impotent, but of good conversation'. In 1551 a grant was made to Walter Farre and Ralph Standysshe, 'Gentlemen, of all that the late chapel or chantry of Billericay in our said county of Essex, now dissolved, by whatsoever other name the same late free chapel or chantry may be called or named' and sundry lands. These two gentlemen, according to the evidence available, appear to have resold the chapel with its lands to one Mr Tyrell, whose family kept the lands and sold the chapel to the inhabitants of Billericay, who appointed feoffees or trustees to maintain the structure and provide at least one service each Sunday as well as appointing their own minister. The chapel still remained under the jurisdiction of the vicar of Great Burstead, however, which meant that formally it was a chapel of ease.

Edward was succeeded on his death in 1553 by his sister Mary, who was a devout Catholic – and while she was on the throne Protestants were persecuted. During the reigns of Protestant monarchs Ingatestone and Stock had retained secret Catholic places of worship at Ingatestone Hall and Crondon Park; Billericay, however, was a rather more Protestant place.

On Mary's death in 1558 she was succeeded by her sister Elizabeth, who was a Protestant. All change … During Elizabeth's reign, which lasted from 1558 to 1603, Catholics were persecuted. Perhaps because of the area's Protestant leanings, there were no Catholic martyrs from Billericay. The nearest known was the Catholic priest John Payne, who served Lady Anne Petre and Ingatestone Hall. He was executed at Chelmsford in 1582.

PROTESTANT MARTYRS OF BILLERICAY

There were six Protestant martyrs from Billericay – but not all were killed. James Harris, the seventeen-year-old servant of William Harris of Little Burstead, and Margaret Ellis of Billericay were arrested and taken before the Bishop of London, Bishop Bonner, by two JPs, Sir John Mordaunt and Sir Edmund Tyrrel. Margaret was delivered up to the two JPs in a letter written to Bishop Bonner, and died in Newgate Prison in late April or early May 1556 while she was awaiting execution. James was accused of not attending the parish church for more than a year. James made a statement, in which he said that out of fear he had once been to church and received the Catholic sacraments; he felt sorry for doing this and detested his actions with all his heart. Bishop Bonner persuaded him to go to confession, which he did, and when he was asked his sins by the priest he said that there were so many that they couldn't be numbered. When the priest reported this to Bishop Bonner, the bishop took James into his garden and savagely whipped him with a stick taken from a cherry tree. The other martyrs were Joan Potter, wife of Hugh Potter, Joan Hornes, Elizabeth Thackwell and Thomas Wattes. Joan Potter and Elizabeth Thackwell were delivered up to the bishop in a letter written to him by the two JPs. Joan Hornes was burned at the stake in May 1556. When asked about her disbelief in the sacrament of communion, she told Bishop Bonner: 'If you can make your God to shed blood or show me any sign of the true living body then I will believe you, but it is bread to substance, and that which you call heresy is the manner in which I trust to serve my God to the end of my days.' She also told him: 'Concerning the bishop and see of Rome I detest them as abominations and desire ever to be delivered from the same.' Thomas Wattes was a linen draper, who was arrested and brought before Lord Rich and then Bishop Bonner and Nicholas Harpsfield, the Archdeacon of Canterbury and Vicar General of London. Despite being urged to recant his faith he refused, and was burned at the stake in Chelmsford in June 1555. Joan Potter and James Harris, although tortured, were not executed.

LIFE AND CRIME:
THE SIXTEENTH CENTURY

During the sixteenth century we find the first reference to a windmill in Billericay: the accounts of Stratford Langthorne Abbey for 1537–8 include a few details of a piece of land named Monipardes near Old Mill Hill and two mills held with it, both in the parish of Great Burstead. A Petre rental (for Cowbridge) of 1563 has a reference to a mill, which in 1593 is known to have been leased by one Thomas Wattes. A map of 1593 shows a watermill at Noak Bridge, but this seems to have been abandoned in favour of a windmill at a different site.

From surviving records quite a bit is known about the market in Billericay in the late sixteenth century. For example, because salt bins are mentioned in a document of 1593 that relates to the Crown Inn, we know that it was split into two sections: a cattle market and a general market. In 1573 Great Burstead manorial court, which controlled Billericay market, ordained that corn and flour dealers could only sell their wares in the town's market, and that sales elsewhere were to incur a penalty of 12d per bushel. Also in 1573 the court decided that anyone who bought and sold butter in the market before the market bell was rung to formally open it should forfeit 5s. To give an example of illegal selling and buying, in 1576 Daniel Wilson of West Thurrock was indicted before the Great Burstead manorial court for buying a whole packhorse-load of butter at Billericay. Wholesalers needed a licence to buy and sell, and in 1578 there was a case of illegal pig-selling when at one of the quarter sessions ten drovers, five butchers, a badger (provisions dealer) and a linen draper bought and sold sixty pigs without licence at Billericay, Romford, Cressing and Ingrave markets and had bought sixty pigs worth 10s each, for resale at a profit. All but six of the drovers were found guilty. In 1582 a miller was warned by court under a penalty of 6s 8d to sell his flour at the market cross of Burstead, which was suggested by F.G. Emmison in *Elizabethan Life: Home, Work and Land* (1976) as an otherwise unrecorded mention of Billericay. When the Essex county magistrates met at

Epiphany in 1596 they had before them the names of twenty-two poulterers and higglers (provision dealers) who bought wares continually at markets and at farmers' houses contrary to their order, and thereby forestalling the Chelmsford, Braintree, Dunmow and Billericay markets.

Information about trades and professions in Billericay at this time can be found in a number of sources. For example, a town map from 1593 names the weavers who were in the town. Court records, both for Church and criminal courts, are also good sources. As an aside, it should be explained that until 1860 the Church exercised a degree of control over the laity, with some offences being tried and sentenced in the Church courts. In the records of Essex Easter Quarter Session Court for 1575 we learn of Marmaduke Middleton, a Billericay schoolmaster 'who greatly disliked his trade and profession', who was indicted as a common brawler and disturber. He appealed to the Privy Council in July, and as a result the Quarter Sessions magistrates wrote to the Assizes judges to conclude the matter. However, Marmaduke failed to appear before the Easter Quarter Session Court and was eventually declared an outlaw. At a Church court in 1596 the Billericay churchwarden presented the schoolmaster Joseph Smith for 'keeping a school not withstanding an approved [i.e. proved] adulterer'; Smith said that he would perform such penance as he was asked to do. It should be explained that the law of the day forebade anyone from teaching without a licence from the Church. We know that there were butchers living in Billericay at this time, as F.G. Emmison in *Elizabethan Life – Disorder* (1970) mentions that at an unspecified date during Elizabeth's reign William Norrys, a Billericay butcher at the market, struck another violently on the head with a quart pot and drew blood. Norrys was also indicted for being a common drunkard. In 1559 and 1560 three tanners and three butchers were before the Great Burstead manorial court for using their 'artifices ill' – in other words, being guilty of bad workmanship. They were fined. F.G. Emmison also wrote about Sir William Petre and Ingatestone Hall, and he mentions in that connection the existence of a cooper in Billericay and a dealer in (if not a maker of) agricultural implements. The surviving records of John Petre, the first Lord Petre, tell us that there was at least one glazier in Billericay.

During this period the manor courts appointed officers to ensure that any bread or ale sold within the manor was of the correct standard. Other goods were sometimes subject to inspection. For example, in 1560 searchers and sealers of leather were elected at Great Burstead; they would have inspected leather products sold in Billericay.

From 1583 there is evidence of a baker or bakers in Billericay, as in that year a baker from the town who sold his bread at the Aveley market was before the courts for making bread that did not accord to the regulations and was unpleasant to eat: 'unwholesome' is the word used. Under a penalty of £3 the baker was ordered to make loaves of the correct size before the last day of the month. He obviously took no notice, or possibly lapsed, as in 1594 the Aveley manorial court fined him 10s, with a double penalty for a further offence.

In 1600 John Joce and Henry Hickson were charged by the courts with selling ale and bread without a licence, despite having been forbidden to do so by Sir John Petre and Mr John Butler.

The Tudor paint shop is the south wing of a sixteenth-/seventeenth-century house. (Basildon Heritage)

From court records we also know that from at least as early as 1560 there were alehouses or tippling houses in Billericay or Great Burstead. In that year at Great Burstead manorial court six 'tipplers of ale' (alehouse keepers) were fined 2d each for selling short measure. In 1585 ten 'tipplers of ale' paid 3d for selling ale in bowls and cups and not in sealed measures. By the end of the century there were five inns: the Crown (which dated from at least 1563), the Swan (1563), the George (1563) and the Red Lion (1593). There was also the Bull, which is known to have existed before 1610; but the building is unnamed on the 1593 town map. It was illegal to keep an alehouse without a licence. At the end of the Elizabethan age, in 1602, an unlicensed alehouse in Great Burstead was presented to the courts. What went on in drinking establishments, whether alehouses or inns, could land licensees in trouble. This happened in 1580, when a Great Burstead victualler was before the courts for allowing 'shovegroat and quoits and such like games which bred evil demeanour'.

Before examining other offences dealt with in the courts, it is worth discussing the police system that existed in those days. The officers of the law were the constables. Unlike today these were not professionals but were elected. The office was only held for a specific time and was a rather

Nos 3, 4 and 6 Norsey Road are sixteenth-century buildings, which are shown on a 1593 map of Billericay. (Author)

poorly paid – and rather unpopular – job: constables were often subject to abuse and ridicule. Their main tasks were to appoint watchmen for the town, parish or manor, to pass vagrants on to the next parish or manor, to raise hue and cry after malefactors and fugitives, to execute justices' warrants for arrest, and to take charge of and repair the archery butts, the stocks, the cage, the whipping post and the ducking stool. The number of constables appointed in a particular manor varied. Great Burstead, including Billericay, had three.

There were many offences either heard in the Great Burstead criminal and civil courts or committed by people from Billericay and heard in other courts. There is only space here to summarise a representative selection, in the hope that they shed light on this aspect of life in the sixteenth century.

In 1557 there was a case of horseshoe stealing before Great Burstead's court leet (the manorial criminal court): on 29 October John Tavernor of Stock was up before the court for taking a shoe worth a penny farthing (1¼d) from the foot of a horse belonging to John Mylles of Billericay. He was found guilty and was fined 4d. In 1600 there was a case of cattle stealing when Henry Jepson, a Billericay blacksmith, and James Slack, a Great Easton husbandman, stole fourteen steers from three people in Billericay.

In 1566 there is a case of breaking and entry: a Laindon labourer was before the courts for breaking into the house of Henry Theedam, a Billericay linen draper.

His penalty is not recorded. The takings were of little value, and included 3lb of raisins and three dozen points (tagged laces). In 1597 a Billericay man and a Laindon woman attacked Thomas Felsted with a dagger at his house in Laindon, stealing £25 in money and some linen. Both were found guilty.

A case of embezzlement in which a Billericay man was the victim was recorded in 1572. John Hamonde of Hornchurch confessed before Edward Rich JP that on the Monday before Whit Sunday he went to Billericay and offered his services to John Daivy, a shoemaker in the town. After a fortnight he was sent to his father, as was the custom, to find out if his father would give permission for him to be apprenticed to Daivy for five years. He didn't go, but hung around outside Billericay. On returning to the town that evening he was taken up by the town watchman, carried to Daivy's house and sent to bed. An hour afterwards Hamonde went to Daivy's chamber, took a purse containing an unknown amount of money out of his hose and 59s 6d from a chest in the chamber, then ran off to South Benfleet and thence over the river to Rochester, where he spent 20s of the money. He was traced to Kent, and brought back to Essex, where he admitted everything in the presence of eight gentlemen. Daivy was bound over to prosecute him at the next Assizes. Unfortunately, according to F.G. Emmison in *Elizabethan Life – Disorder* (1970), the file for that assize is missing. This case suggests that Billericay had only one town watchman on duty on the night of the robbery. He clearly did not feel it necessary to keep Hamonde in custody for the night, then hand him over the next day to the parish constables of Great Burstead.

In 1576 there was a case that not only involves common assault but also the use of threats. At Michaelmas in 1573 Matthew Bell of Ramsden Bellhouse hired six milch cows from John Crushe of Laindon for three years at an annual rent of 20s. Their return at the end of the period, or the payment of 33s 4d for any cow that was not returned, was guaranteed by a bond given by Bell and John Knightbridge of Laindon. Edmund Croxon, who was Bell's son-in-law, tried on many occasions to get Crushe to give him the bond and promised to deliver the stock, explaining that he had to sue Bell for unpaid legacies and would make him unable to recompense for the cows; further, he stated that Knightbridge was worth nothing. Croxon also gave this message to Crushe's wife on two occasions. One day at sunset Crushe went to Croxon's house to fetch some of his hay, and was called into the house by Croxon's wife. When Crushe went into the parlour Croxon struck him down with a short crabtree staff, and swore by God's blood that he would thrust his dagger into him.

That evening John Nevell of Laindon went to Crushe's house on behalf of Croxon, and asserted that Crushe had injured Croxon, who demanded damages. Nevell then drew Crushe into a field by arrangement with Croxon, who told Crushe that he had lost £5 by coming to his house. Nevell added that Crushe should give Croxon recompense. Crushe denied having injured him, but was finally terrified by the situation. He offered Coxon an oak tree to make amends, but this was refused: Croxon answered that he would not accept all the oak trees that Crushe had. Crushe asked what he wanted, and Croxon replied the bond – suggesting that Crushe should deliver this to Nevell the following morning. Crushe did as instructed. Shortly afterwards, when Crushe was riding to market, Croxon accosted him in the highway with a hedging bill and swore that he and Nevell would 'misuse' him. The upshot was that Crushe submitted a complaint to court, seeking redress for the safety of his life. The result is not known.

In 1581 John Potter of Tye Common, convicted of manslaughter at the county Assizes, was freed by one of the queen's general pardons. When anyone was hanged not only was their life forfeited but their land and their goods also; either to the sovereign or to the lord of the manor, if the right forfeiture was attached to the manor. This caused a dilemma for the manor of Great Burstead, which had the right to hanged persons' goods: Potter had been pardoned by the queen but in the law's eyes was guilty. Should the manor be allowed to keep his estate? The matter was referred back to the county Assizes court.

At the Trinity Session of the Assizes in 1582 Agnes Bryant, who sometimes lived in Great Burstead and sometimes in Billericay, was accused of witchcraft. Her indictment was that she bewitched twenty 'brewinges of beere' belonging to Gabriel Bee, by reason of which the beer 'wolde not worke and sporge'. She pleaded not guilty, but was found guilty. Her punishment is not recorded. In May 1590 Agnes Berry, a widow from Great Burstead, was before the courts charged with being a witch. This was on the grounds that her daughter had been accused of incontinency – that is, having sex outside marriage.

In 1559 William Seymer of Billericay was before the manorial court at Ramsden Crays for grazing his cattle on the common there, when he had no right to do so. Sometimes animals were impounded by the lord of the manor, for any number of reasons, and the owner of the animals was fined if he forcibly attempted to take them back. In 1582 a man who drove his cattle from the Great Burstead manorial pound, where they had been put after trespassing on the lord's wood, had to find 6s 8d.

This timber-framed house dates from 1577. (Author)

North Sea House was 55 High Street, of Tudor origin and at one time the Anchor Inn. (Basildon Heritage)

In the Manorial Court Rolls of 1585 we find a case involving non-payment for a hay crop. Thomas Fuller the elder, a Great Burstead yeoman is quoted as saying: 'William Bryckett oweth me for the first crop of my More Meadow to be taken off by midsummer 14s, and John Norrys butcher oweth me 23s for the first crop of grass to be taken off one meadow lying on the backside of my house at Billericay by the Feast of St John the Baptist next.'

Two Great Burstead men were before the Chafford Hundred 'inquisition' at Horndon-on-the-Hill in 1566 for having received and taken into service a man who had not produced his certificate or testimonial. The trade in which they were engaged is not made clear.

In 1588 Great Burstead manorial court found that three cottages built by two tenants at Hobsters Corner and Norsey Corner were to be pulled down. However, the inhabitants of Great Burstead had built a new house for one Thomas Jackson and his wife, who was then deceased, and begged the lord of the manor to allow it to remain for the use of the parish with a rent of 1d a year. Nothing further is heard of this; it is suggested that the parish might have wanted to use the house for pauper families.

A young man, Thomas Carr of Billericay, was before the courts in 1600 for living idly, following no trade and spending his time going from alehouse to alehouse.

Great Burstead manorial court passed a decree in 1573: 'No person dwelling within the town [Billericay] or elsewhere shall cut any timber or trees in the lord's wood called Norsey or elsewhere within the demesne or on their own lands without licence under paid of 10s or being imprisoned for twenty-four hours as may seem the better to the officers.'

Also in 1573 the manorial court passed a decree to the effect that all who dwelt at South Green should put their washing stool (dirty water) in an appropriate place, so that the filthy water didn't run into the flood ditch. In 1588 the manorial court decreed that anyone in Billericay or Great Burstead who made a dung hill in the market-place or Church Street and allowed it to remain there for more than one month should forfeit 3s 4d. In 1590 two tenants were told to clear away the dunghills behind the chapel (this was the chapel of ease in Billericay High Street, the current St Mary Magdalen). In the same year the manorial court censured all those who cast their pits (dirty water) into the spring.

In 1581 Great Burstead manorial court forbade the letting of tenements to any person who was a sub-tenant without the consent of ten or eight of the chief inhabitants. In 1588 the manor forbade the inhabitants of the manor from putting strangers into their houses 'by which the parishioners be charged without the consent of eight inhabitants'. In 1591 this was amended to 'six honest or chief inhabitants', and in 1598 to 'the inhabitants'.

Every copyholder of property within a manor or his lessee was bound to keep dwelling and outhouses in repair at his own expense, and to the satisfaction of the lord of the manor. If this was not fulfilled penalties were imposed. In the Great Burstead manor court in 1591, after a tenant's death, a jury decided that his dwelling and garden fence were 'in great decay'. The fearsome penalty of £5 was imposed on his son and heir, should he not remedy the defects quickly.

To explain copyhold, mentioned in the previous paragraph: this was a system of landholding according to the custom of the manor. Title deeds were originally a copy of the record of the manorial court. There were two main kinds of copyhold tenure. There was Copyhold of Inheritance, where a single tenant landholder paid rent and was liable to perform duties for the lord of the manor. When he died the holding normally passed to his heir. There was also Copyhold for Lives, in which three named persons were nominated copyholders. The first was the holder tenant, who held the property for the duration of his life. The other two were said to be 'in reversion and remainder', and effectively formed a queue.

In the second half of the sixteenth century a duty called a suit of court was imposed on all males above a certain age living in a manor. The age varied from place to place, and could be twelve, fourteen, fifteen or sixteen. Not every male who was required to pay did so. Normally defaulters were fined, but there were also a number of 'essoins', or excuses, made. At the Great Burstead court in 1559 essoins were submitted by twenty-four tenants.

During the sixteenth century archery practice was compulsory. In Billericay the butts used were at South Green. It seems that in 1577 people were in the habit of using the green for grazing their cattle: 'Those who dwell around South Green and others who used to put their cattle on it henceforth put no cattle on it on Sundays or feast days in the afternoon between Easter and Michaelmas, because it is a hindrance and nuisance to the bowmen who of old shoot on the green.'

Finally in our selection of criminal and civil cases, and as we reflect on crime and punishment in these distant times, it is worth thinking about the day-to-day fate of those who overstepped the mark in a society that punished through public humiliation and sometimes other physical abuse. In 1584 an order was made by Great Burstead manorial court, ordering the inhabitants of Billericay to repair their pillory. The following year the inhabitants of the manor of Great Burstead asked leave to make both their pillory and cucking (or ducking) stool good before the next court was held.

Turning now to the ecclesiastical courts, which tended to concern moral offences and operated under canon law, we discover immediately that they had no right to impose fines or to physically harm anyone brought before them. One form of punishment that they could inflict was penance – where the offender had to wear a white robe and carry a white rod in his hand, often in front of the whole congregation and sometimes outside the church. This occurred in 1566, when a Great Burstead man who condoned his wife's alleged adultery had to suffer in his church and in Brentwood market, with his fault written on his back in large letters.

In 1575 Geoffrey Cole of Great Burstead was before the Church court, because 'on Twelfthtide last' he was 'abroad with others a mumming and being late abroad midnight, lying upon a bed in Sweting's house, Magdalen Wade was found sitting upon the bed, but no evil committed as he saith'. As to who the witness for the prosecution was the records do not say; neither is the punishment recorded.

In 1576 a Billericay woman penitently confessed and promised amendment before the vicar and twelve honest men of the parish of Billericay in the church after the sermon. The church official who directed this seems to have forgotten that Billericay was not a parish but a chapelry of Great Burstead. What the woman did wrong is not known. In the same year Joan Cooper of Great Burstead, a slanderer of her neighbours, hung a horn on the fence of one Parker, apparently with no evil intent. She had to confess in church with the horn slung upon her sleeve. The horn was emblematic of power, and came to be regarded as symbolic of a proud, pushy and domineering character. To make horns at someone was to hold your fist to the head with two fingers extended like a pair of horns; it was an insulting gesture. Also in 1576 Marmaduke Middleton, mentioned earlier, was up before the court of the Archdeacon of Essex for living with a woman called Alice who was not his wife, and causing a great disturbance to his neighbours. Disputing the charge, he was asked to find four men to plead for him. Things didn't go quite as planned. One of the four witnesses he found refused to swear, but Marmaduke was given a second chance. The churchwardens then said that he was suspected of committing adultery with Margery, the wife of James Parker, a charge that Marmaduke denied. Margery Parker was also cited, but she did not turn up. Marmaduke found no one to swear for him, and was ordered to wear the white penitential robe in Great Burstead church.

Unmarried maidservants who became pregnant or were found to be living in sin not only usually suffered dismissal as well as having to do public penance in church, but some also became liable to arrest under the vagrancy laws. In 1599 Sarah Eyon of Great Burstead and formerly of Mountnessing, the maidservant of Thomas Folkes of Mountnessing, had lived 'in whoredom' with a fellow servant Thomas Hopkins. Hopkins had left the country and Eyon had been dismissed, but neither received a punishment other than Eyon being sent back to Great Burstead.

Those who passed on sexually transmitted diseases could also end up before the Church courts. In 1588 Thomas Robertes suffered this fate, having infected his wife. The penalty was reserved.

It was a crime in the eyes of the Church for the unmarried to live together, and also a crime for the married not to live together. In 1583 Thomas Finch of Great Burstead found himself up before the Church court because his wife was not living with him. He explained that the fault was not with him but with his wife, for while he was content to live with her she had left him – and he did not know where she had gone.

After the Reformation, apart from during the reign of Queen Mary, Sunday attendance at divine service in the Church of England was compulsory. Non-attendance could mean a summons to court. In 1599 John Burrowes appeared, because he was 'a misordered fellow and cometh not to church and [was] a common drunkard and blasphemer'. In 1600 the churchwardens of Great Burstead (Henry Weler and another) were before the courts for refusing to hear divine service from William Simons, who was appointed reader in the absence of the vicar William Pease. Even your behaviour in church could lead to your appearance before the Church courts. In 1583 John Turnar and Augustine Wattes, both of Great Burstead, were charged with obstinately refusing to kneel when receiving communion. Both replied that they had thought Christ gave communion while seated, but as they had received better instruction since they now received it kneeling.

On 14 June 1599 there was a case of sheep-stealing by a Billericay churchwarden and another person. This was heard by the Church courts at Great Baddow. It was reported that for a long time forty ewes had belonged to the church or chapel at Billericay, which were used to provide relief for the poor. Profits from the sale of wool and meat were used to buy beer, bread and cheese.

No. 110 High Street was of late sixteenth-century origin. It was demolished in 1960. (Basildon Heritage)

The Chequers, which dates back to the late sixteenth century. (Basildon Heritage)

John Warly of Billericay with Robert Attridge of Kent disposed of the sheep contrary to the wishes of the person who had donated the sheep originally, and thus robbed the poor of their due. The sentence is not recorded.

Moving on from court proceedings to other legal matters, a source that can add much colour to the distant past is wills. Bequests always make interesting reading. Some of those made by people in the Billericay/ Great Burstead area in Elizabethan times appear on the face of it to be extraordinary, but were presumably entirely sensible at the time. For example, the 1585 will of Thomas Fuller the elder, the Great Burstead yeoman mentioned above, bequeathed to his wife 'three load of billet' – that is short, thick pieces of wood, probably firewood. Stephen Clarke, a Billericay woollen draper made his will in 1589, and bequeathed to his son-in-law 'my brown cow with her calf by her side, if God prosper it'. This is evidence that even poorer people kept livestock. John Jones, a Billericay schoolmaster, showed concern for the religious welfare of his children in his will, dated 1599. He left his widow the residue of property on condition that she brought up 'my children in the fear of God as my trust is as a faithful matron'. Another person to mention his children in his will is Thomas Thorpe, a minister who lived in Great Burstead. In 1570 he wrote: 'I will that Mr Hawkyne minister shall pay unto his son Thomas Hawkyne the 6s 8d that he oweth me for schooling.' William Lyncolne, also of Great Burstead, provided for his wife in his will of 1560 'in the name of her jointure, because she shall not claim the third of none of my lands and house, every year 40s'. (Jointure is provision for a wife after the death of her husband.)

In a will of 1563 there is a case of a Billericay woman who received a bequest from a stranger she was caring for. Richard Page, 'late soldier at Newehaven [in Flanders] and now living in Billericay', gave 20s 'to Mundayes' woman that doth keep me while I am here'.

In those days weapons or tools used in particular trades were often passed down in wills. Thomas Thorp, who was a minister but not the vicar of Great Burstead, included his dagger among his bequests; his will is dated 1570. Andrew Brette, a wheelwright of Great Burstead, left his son Edward 'an almain rivet with a bill thereunto belonging' in his will of 1582.

THE SPANISH ARMADA

The Spanish Armada of 1588 was a major event during the Elizabethan period, and affected much of the country. Preparations were made to counter any potential invasion, and this included the formation of a pioneer corps, which was armed with billhooks, scythes and pitchforks. Commanding officers had to stay in their counties and ensured that their men could turn out at an hour's notice. To stop any acts of sabotage, provost marshals were appointed to round up vagabonds and other suspicious persons. Warning beacons were built on hills; one is known to have been located in Stock. At the first sighting of enemy ships these were to be fired and church bells were to be rung, as an indication that men should muster under the lord lieutenants or their deputies at their rallying points (often the beacons). Plans were discussed for cutting and flooding roads, and the adoption of a scorched earth policy. Horsemen, some heavily armed, were instructed to move livestock, to prevent its capture by the enemy. Mercifully, as on later occasions when there was a threat of invasion, all these preparations were not needed.

Defence was everything. Even in peacetime all men between fifteen and fifty had to serve in the militia, which was a military body set up to preserve internal order or defend the locality against an invader – in other words a standing auxiliary army. The militia was supposed to be regularly mustered for training purposes, but in reality this happened rarely – and local regiments could not be relied on to serve outside their own counties. From a document we know that the total number of eligible men in Billericay and Great Burstead in 1539 was sixty-nine. They were also liable for service in the *posse commitatus* – an *ad hoc* body that was gathered together by a law officer to apprehend lawbreakers.

five

PURITANS, THE *MAYFLOWER* AND CIVIL WAR

Following the Reformation two strands of Protestantism developed. There was the sort developed within the Church of England, which can be described as Protestantism with elements of Catholicism. Secondly there was a more extreme version, which took the view that the Bible alone was the authority for faith and for the practice of religion. The followers of this version questioned anything that hinted at Catholic ceremony or ritual; we know them as Puritans. They were quite numerous in Billericay.

Although Billericay was part of the parish of Great Burstead, its inhabitants had the right to appoint their own minister to conduct services and preach. They maintained him financially, but his appointment was subject to the approval of the incumbent of Great Burstead, who had overall responsibility for the whole parish and seems to have lived in Billericay, as this was where most of his parishioners lived. There wasn't always a minister for the chapel, but when there was one he appears to have been a semi-independent curate. In 1594 the people of Billericay appointed Thomas Stoughton to the post of curate; he was Puritan in his persuasions.

The Lord of the Manor at this time was Edwin Riche, the brother of Robert Lord Riche, later 1st Earl of Warwick. The Essex manors of the Riches' father had been divided between his sons on his death in 1580, but Edwin was only a minor at the time and his brother seems to have managed his affairs. Robert Riche was a Puritan, but because the right of appointment of the next vicar of Great Burstead had been acquired by a yeoman, Henry Hamond, who was a follower of orthodox Church of England Protestantism, there was nothing Robert Riche could do about who was appointed vicar. In 1596 William Pease was appointed to the post. Pease was acceptable to the Archbishop of Canterbury, Archbishop Whitgift, who ratified the appointment. It should have been the Bishop of London who did this, as Great Burstead was in his diocese, but the bishopric of London was vacant.

In 1600 the living of Coggeshall became vacant, and Lord Rich appointed Stoughton to it. His views were rather too radical, however, and he was deprived of the living in 1606.

Pease had the job ministering to all in the parish of Great Burstead: both those who did and those who did not follow the Church of England's teaching. Not everybody was regular in their attendance, and there was little the vicar and his churchwardens could do except threaten excommunication. Pease seems to have been rather good at keeping the Puritans in check – and on one occasion he apparently boxed the ears of Puritan children. He wasn't always successful, though. In 1612 Master Hill, a clergyman of Great Burstead who had Puritan views and may have been appointed by the people of Billericay to serve in the chapel, was hauled before the archdeacon's court for not following the Book of Common Prayer's stricture to make the sign of the cross during the ceremony of baptism. He was required to do so in future.

It was also in 1612, at Easter at the celebration of Holy Communion, that a Christopher Martin, who was one of the churchwardens, first expressed Puritan views. At the Easter service all parishioners were expected to receive Holy Communion, and to kneel to receive it. Christopher Martin and his fellow churchwarden John Weald refused to do so, preferring to stand. Christopher Martin and John Weald were taken before the archdeacon's court. It appears that Martin's offence was based on conviction, but Weald seems just to have been following Martin.

Apart from Master Hill and Christopher Martin, there were other Puritans who caused Pease trouble. Nicholas Weald was presented before the archdeacon's court for telling his son who was preparing for confirmation to tell Pease that his father gave him his name, and asking if he would have him lie and whether a lie was a sin, and also for refusing to send his maid to be catechised. James Salmon, Robert Salmon and Thomas Picle were also summoned before the archdeacon's court for similar reasons.

Because of his connection with the *Mayflower*, Christopher Martin can be held to be Billericay's most famous citizen. No one knows where he was born or even when. He is reputed to have lived in the building that is now the Kosthuree Indian restaurant, although this has not been proved. The first thing we know about him is that on 26 February 1606 he married Marie Prowe, a widow with a son by her first marriage, named Solomon. We know Christopher's trade, for also in 1606 he was up before the Quarter Sessions on 2 July, when George Hills, a mercer (linen draper) of Great Burstead, gave evidence against, among

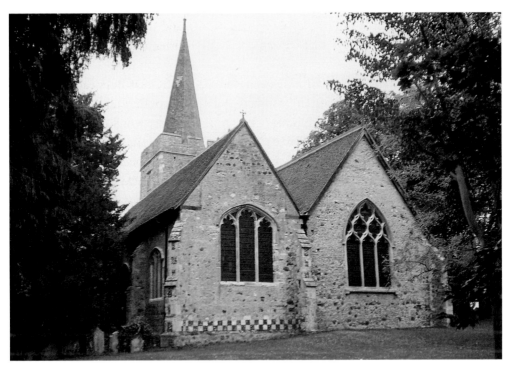

Great Burstead parish church, where Christopher Martin first made his stand for Puritanism. (Author)

others, Christopher Martin of the same trade, for practising the trade without being apprenticed to it. This was in contravention of the Statute of Apprentices of 1563, which required all persons practising a trade to have served an apprenticeship of seven years. The penalty for not complying with this was 40s a month.

After this brush with the law nothing much seems to have happened to suggest that Christopher Martin was anything other than a respectable citizen of seventeenth-century Billericay. In 1609 he had a son by Marie, christened Nathaniel on 26 February that year in Great Burstead church. Also in that year he was one of the two substantial holders of property who were required to attend the archdeacon's visitation with the churchwardens to confirm the state of the parish church. Two years later, at the Easter vestry meeting, he was elected a churchwarden: it was his turn, as a prominent citizen of the community. In the same year, 1611, Martin's business seems to have prospered, or he obtained capital to expand it. The Great Burstead manorial court rolls reveal that he had acquired three properties in Billericay by this time, one of which was divided into two tenements. Two of the properties were across the road from what is

The Chantry House, *c.*1955. (Basildon Heritage)

now the Chantry Café, and this is probably why the suggestion that he lived in that building arose. He was formally admitted to the properties by the normal practice, being invested with the copyhold tenure at the manorial court in May 1612. One of the occupants of the buildings was William Pease. Perhaps a dispute arose between Pease and Martin regarding Pease's tenancy, causing Martin to express Puritan views because of personal animosity.

The business over taking communion wasn't the only matter that caused Martin to be summoned before the archdeacon's court; he also failed to present the church accounts, precipitating another hearing. After this little more is heard of him for some time. We know he was present at the annual court baron (manorial civil court) from 1613 to 1617 as a member of the jury, but that is all. In both 1618 and 1619 Martin was absent and sent his apologies.

In 1620 Martin was up before the archdeacon's court again, this time in connection with the vicar's preparation of children for confirmation. Martin's crime – and this is familiar territory, as so many other Billericay people had offended in similar manner – was to make his son answer William Pease that his father gave him his name, and not his godparents at his baptism. According to the Catechism of the Church of England, as contained in the *Book of Common*

Prayer, to be learned by everyone who was going to be confirmed, the first two questions were 'What is your name?' and 'Who gave you that name?' The reply to the second was supposed to be 'My Godfathers and Godmothers in my Baptism; wherein I was made a member of Christ, the child of Christ and an inheritor of the kingdom of heaven.' Puritans argued that this did not have Biblical authority.

The first we hear of Christopher Martin's involvement in emigration to America is in the records of the Virginia Company of London for 15 January 1616, which records that Bills of Adventure were allowed to Captain Raphe Hamor and 'all persons hereunder named for every man transported at their charge being 16 who were to have no bond'. The allowance for every person to be transported was £12 10s. Seven persons had ventured their capital: Captain Hamor received an allowance for five persons, Thomas Hamor for four, William Tucker for two and Robert Sturton, John Blachall and Elias Roberts for one. For the remaining two the allowance of £25 was to Christopher Martin. According to R.J. Carpenter in *Christopher Martin, Great Burstead and the Mayflower* (1982), American scholars regard this Christopher Martin as the same person who was the treasurer of the *Mayflower*.

The Virginia Company was chartered in 1606 by Queen Elizabeth I's successor, King James I of England and VI of Scotland, for the purpose of colonising America. It was named in honour of Elizabeth – the Virgin Queen. It had two divisions: the Virginia Company of London and the Virginia Company of Plymouth.

The memorial tablet to Christopher Martin at Great Burstead church. (Author)

In about 1620 Christopher Martin decided to emigrate: why is not known. It could be argued that getting involved with the emigration movement and actually emigrating himself were the same thing. Not so. It was quite possible for someone to be involved in helping those who wanted to go to America, while deciding to remain in England himself.

It is possible that Christopher Martin decided to emigrate because he got fed up with Billericay and England, and decided to go to a place where he could practise his Puritan religion freely and without hindrance. In May 1620 he acquired shares in the Virginia Company of London from Captain George Percy, the son of Sir Henry Percy, 8th Earl of Northumberland, who had gone out with an expedition in 1606. He was appointed governor of the colony in 1609, but returned to England in 1612. It was now that a route to emigration presented itself to Christopher Martin. Here a little background is necessary. At this time the Virginia Company of London was looking for ways to encourage settlers to its plantations, and was courting the Brownist community in Leyden, in the Netherlands. The Brownists were Puritans who had fled their native Lincolnshire to gain freedom of worship. Without going too far into the history of the Netherlands, it is sufficient to say that they foresaw problems in maintaining their independence and were beginning to contemplate the establishment of a community in America. The Virginia Company saw the Brownists as a labour force that would help them to gain a return on the capital that they had invested. Before they were able to join forces, the Brownists had to seek reconciliation with the King of England – and this was done through a series of delicate political negotiations. In due course the Brownists wavered in their talks with the Virginia Company, and entered into negotiations with the New Netherlands Company, before finally taking a third way. Thomas Weston, a London ironmonger, arrived on the scene with promises of financial backing from friends, and draft articles of agreement were prepared for the removal of the Brownists to Virginia. Soon it became obvious that the numbers of those from the Leyden community in the first ships had to be supplemented, and somehow our Christopher Martin was chosen to represent the so-called 'strangers', those from outside the Brownite community who were travelling to America. The fact that he was a Puritan helped, of course.

William Bradford, who sailed with the Pilgrim Fathers as they are known and was governor of the Plymouth colony for most of the time from 1621 to 1656, wrote the following in his history of the colony: 'For besides those two formerly mentioned sent from Leyden for this end, viz Mr [John] Carver and

Robert Cushman, there was one chosen in England to be joined with them for to make the provisions for the voyage; his name was Mr Martin, he came from Billericay in Essex, from which parts came sundry others to go with them, as also from London and other places.' Martin's role was not merely that of strangers' representative; he also acted as the Virginia Company's agent and the project's treasurer.

Unfortunately, early in the proceedings Martin showed an obstinacy that later made him unpopular with his fellow travellers. He made his own mind up and didn't listen to other opinions. To give an example, on 10 June 1620 Robert Cushman wrote from London to John Carver: 'You wrote to Mr Martin, to prevent the making of the provisions in Kent, which he did, and set down his resolution how much would have of everything, without respect to any council or exception.'

Added to Martin's responsibilities was the role of governor of the *Mayflower*. The Pilgrims eventually embarked at Southampton in two ships, the *Mayflower* (or *May Flower* as it was probably called) and the *Speedwell*. According to William Bradford, with Martin were his wife and two servants, Solomon Prowe (his stepson) and John Langemore. There is no mention of Nathaniel Martin, which makes one wonder what happened to him. Death? I can find no record of it. Perhaps he decided to stay with relatives in England.

The financial affairs of the company were so mismanaged that in August 1620 they were forced to raise £100 before leaving Southampton 'to clear things at their going away'. 'After that, Robert Cushman, Mr Peirce and Mr Martin brought them into a better form and wrote them in a book ...' Because of leaks the *Speedwell* twice had to return to port, once to Dartmouth and once to Plymouth – where it was abandoned. The *Mayflower* finally set off alone. Martin's obstinacy continued. During the return to Dartmouth it had been found that half the provisions for the voyage would be eaten before the Pilgrims left Britain, and when they got to America they would not have a month's supply left. Robert Cushman asked Martin about this, but he could not and would not give account of what had happened to the supplies, nor would he supply the accounts. On 17 August Robert Cushman wrote to Edward Southwark:

Nearly £700 has been bestowed at [South]Hampton, upon I know not. Mr Martin said he neither can nor will give any account of it, and if he be called upon for accounts he cries out of unthankfulness for his pains and care, that we are suspicious of him, and flings away and will end nothing. Also he so insults our poor

The *Mayflower* on Billericay's town sign. (Author)

people, with such scorn and contempt. It would break your heart to see his dealing and the mourning of our people. They complain to me, and alas! I can do nothing for them; if I speak to him, he flies in my face as mutinous, and says no complaints shall be heard or received but by himself, and says they are forward and waspish and discontented people and I do ill to hear them. There are others who would loose all they have put in, or make satisfaction for what they have had, that they might depart; but he will not hear them, nor suffer them to go ashore, less they should run away. The sailors are also so offended at his ignorant boldness, in meddling and controlling in things he knows not what belongs to, as that some threaten to mischief him, others say they will leave the ship and go their way. But at the best this comes of it, that he makes himself a scorn and laughing stock unto them … And Mr Martin, he said, he never received no money on these conditions, he was not beholden to the merchants for a pine, they were bloodsuckers and I know not what. Simple man, he indeed never made any conditions with the merchants, nor ever spoke with them. But did all that money fly to Hampton, or was it his own? Who will go and lay out money so rashly and lavishly as he did, and never know how he comes by it, or on what conditions? Secondly I told him of the alterations long ago and he was content; but now he dominates and said I had betrayed them into the hands of slaves; he is not beholden to them, he can set out two ships himself to voyage. When good man? He has but £50 in and if he should give up his accounts he would not have a penny left him, as I am persuaded, and friend if we ever make a plantation, God works a miracle.

The 'alterations long ago' refer to the decision made by the Virginia Company of Plymouth to petition the crown for permission to reorganise its affairs, thereby obtaining an undisputed title to the northern half of the territory in its original grant of land. They hoped to please the king by an application to rename it New England. Both Thomas Weston and the Brownist leaders came to favour this, but when the change was made a number of the original adventurers and pilgrims withdrew from the venture. Weston also insisted on a revision of the initial agreement. Originally the settlers were to have two days a week to themselves, but the revised agreement deleted this. Secondly all capital and profits were to be divided equally between adventures and planters at the end of the seven-year term. The pilgrims objected to this, as it would have included their own homes and gardens. Weston continued to insist on the changes, which is what Cushman refers to in the letter above. Martin would have been aware of these developments when he was provisioning the ship, and his attitude suggests that he felt threatened by them.

Eventually the *Mayflower* reached America. Martin and his family were not destined to stay long. Solomon Prowse died on Christmas Eve 1620, and Christopher Martin himself on 6 January 1621. His wife and servant died not long afterwards.

One would love to know Christopher Martin's version of events during the preparation for and during the voyage to America, but sadly he left no record that has survived.

There is a minor sequel to all this. Joseph Hills, the son of George Hills who accused Martin of trading as a mercer without serving an apprenticeship, was one of the first people to follow him to America. Others from Billericay and Great Burstead also went to America. A certain Ralph Hill from the area was one of those responsible for the founding of Billerica, Massachusetts, in 1655.

Although a bit out of context in terms of time, it is worth mentioning that there is also a Billericay in Australia, indicating that settlers travelled in that direction as well at some point (whether of their own free will or under duress has yet to be established!) I have not been able to find out when it was founded.

Meanwhile in Billericay the Rev. Mr Pease soldiered on until he died in 1640. Following his demise the number of Puritan sects in Billericay multiplied. Pease's successor as vicar of Great Burstead was Samuel Bridge, who was instituted into the living in 1641. Bridge was of Puritan persuasion, but he seems to have had problems with the rather more extreme Puritans. In 1646 a militant group entered the chapel and attempted to quarrel with the preacher, the Rev. Samuel Smyth of Hutton, and the congregation. Some of the mob were arrested, and were fined 40s. The sect held open meetings, calling for religious toleration and the abolition of anti-Puritan laws. A group of townspeople petitioned the Quarter Sessions in Chelmsford, explaining that in view of the anarchy and confusion likely to overcome the town, something should be done to prevent the spreading of wicked opinions and violence – so that they could worship in peace. Unfortunately the petition didn't achieve much, as later that year a riot occurred in the chapel. A mob burst in immediately after the sermon and abused the preacher and congregation. Those responsible were fined £2.

In 1642 the English Civil Wars broke out: there were three, lasting from 1642 to 1646, 1648 to 1649 and 1649 to 1651. They were a series of armed conflicts and political machinations between Parliamentarians and Royalists. The Parliamentarians opposed the king (Charles I, successor to James I) who claimed absolute power and the divine right of kings; that is, he saw himself as answerable to no one but God. King Charles I was captured and executed in 1649. His successor was his eldest son, who became King Charles II. The third war ended with a Parliamentary victory at the Battle of Worcester on 3 September 1651. Most Parliamentarians appear to have sought a constitutional monarchy in place of the absolutist monarchy sought by Charles I, but at the end of the second civil war republican leaders such as Oliver Cromwell were in a strong position to abolish the monarchy completely and establish the republican Commonwealth, which lasted from 1649 to 1660, when the monarchy under King Charles II was restored. The main event in the civil wars in which Billericay had a role, albeit a minor one, was the siege of Colchester in 1648. On 1 June of that year the Parliamentarian general Lord Fairfax defeated Royalist troops at Maidstone. The defeated Royalists then headed towards London, crossed the Thames at Greenwich and began to march through Essex. On 12 June they reached Colchester. Meanwhile the Parliamentarians set off in pursuit, crossing the Thames at Tilbury. Having spent the night of 10 June at Billericay they marched to Colchester, which they reached on 13 June. The siege of Colchester lasted from mid-June to late August, when the Royalists surrendered. Unfortunately we do not know where the Parliamentarian troops spent their night at Billericay. Besides those marching to besiege Colchester there seem to have been other troops in the Billericay area during 1648, as the parish registers of Great Burstead in that year record the burials of soldiers and strangers.

One person from the Billericay area is known to have held an officer's position during the wars. Colonel Henry Farre of Burstead was something of a fickle character – first on the Parliamentary side, but later becoming a Royalist. He took part in the Siege of Colchester, and was one of those who surrendered to the Parliamentarian forces. Sentenced to death by firing squad, he managed to escape.

During the time of the Commonwealth those ministers who were loyal to the rites of the Church of England were often removed or, as it was termed, 'sequestrated', and in many churches Puritan ministers carried on the services. Samuel Bridge, being of Puritan persuasion, was able to continue in post. Catholics, of course, still had to worship in secret in private houses.

With the Restoration of the monarchy in 1660 things went the other way. Adherence to the Church of England was compulsory, and under the Corporation Act of 1661 membership of town corporations was not allowed for anyone who would not take the sacrament according to the rites of the Church of England. In 1662 the Act of Uniformity was passed, compelling every Church of England minister to declare their unfeigned assent and consent to everything contained in the Book of Common Prayer. As a result of this between 114 and 116 clergymen were ejected from their livings in Essex. Samuel Bridge had died the previous year, a few months after the Restoration, and so was saved the ignominy of being thus removed.

The non-conformists, as we shall now call them, didn't go away. In 1672 King Charles II issued the Royal Declaration of Indulgence as a gesture of conciliation. Under this, non-conformists were allowed to meet in public places of worship, but only after the place of worship and the teacher had been licensed. Before this, non-conformists had been forced to meet in secret, often at midnight and in places like Mill Hill Woods and the preaching cross – a boundary mark in Goatsmoor Lane. That same year the Rev. Nathaniel Ranew, who was formerly the vicar of Felstead and came to Billericay in 1663 after being ejected from Felstead under the Act of Uniformity, obtained a licence to worship in the house of one Mr Finch in Billericay (now Ask Italian restaurant, 91 High Street) and another licence to worship in the Outwood Common area. However the following year the Indulgence was revoked by Parliament, and under the Sacramental Test Act of 1673 every holder of civil or military office had to receive communion according to the rites of the Church of England and make a declaration against transubstantiation. This latter was a measure against Catholics more than anyone else; they still had

The preaching cross, Goatsmoor Lane. (Author)

No. 91 High Street: the first meeting place of Billericay's dissenters. (Author)

The plaque on 91 High Street, which commemorates its role in Billericay's dissenting history. (Author)

to worship in private houses. However, non-conformists also got caught up by the act. A way round it was known as 'occasional conformity', by which a non-conformist could qualify for office by partaking in communion according to the Church of England just once a year – otherwise being free to protest against the Church.

Real toleration did not come until the Toleration Act of 1689, which granted non-conformist congregations a measure of legal recognition. They were then able to worship freely in their own meeting houses, provided that they were registered with either civil or diocesan authorities. The majority of registrations were made to the courts of Quarter Sessions. There were still outbreaks of religious violence, however. In 1691 a large group of non-conformists broke into Billericay chapel, where a service was being held behind locked doors. They removed the Book of Common Prayer and the vicar's surplice, and did considerable damage to the fittings.

By the end of the seventeenth century non-conformists were worshipping in a barn in what is now Chapel Street but in those days was Wellfield Lane. In 1692 we find the earliest reference to their burial ground site, in the form of an indenture dated 2 July between John James, a baker, and his wife Rebecca, who sold the property to George Bayly the elder of Mountnessing; £50 was paid to John James and 21s to Rebecca.

In 1693 the trustees of the chapel of St John the Baptist decided to hand over their responsibilities to the Bishop of London. It wasn't known whether the building had ever been consecrated, so the bishop came down to Billericay on 8 October to put matters straight. The chapel was dedicated to St Mary Magdalen, with 'all the usual privileges belonging to ancient chapels, but reserving to the Mother Church of Great Burstead all her rights'. The trustees still remained the trustees, though, and did not lose their power of patronage.

SOME MORE ABOUT THE *MAYFLOWER*

While quite a lot has been written about Christopher Martin and his involvement with the *Mayflower* settlers, what of the *Mayflower* herself? She was a three-mast, square-rigged lateen-mizzen ship. She was built somewhere in England, probably in the early seventeenth century, as the earliest mention of her is in records dating from 1606. She was about 90ft long and 26ft wide. She had four decks and a carrying capacity of 180 tons, while her crew was between twenty and thirty men. Her home port was probably Southampton, although that has not been proved. Normally she was engaged in taking wool and hides from England to France and returning with wine and brandy. After her voyage to America with the Pilgrim Father the *Mayflower* returned to England in 1621. The last mention of her is in 1624, when the ship was ruinous and valued at just over £128. Because of its bad condition, the *Mayflower* was almost certainly broken up, the remains being sold off as scrap.

The captain of the *Mayflower* was Christopher Jones, who was also one of the ship's owners. He was born in about 1570 in Maldon, the son of Christopher and Sybil Jones. In 1593 he married Sarah Twitt from Harwich, who died in 1603. He subsequently married Josian Grey, the widow of Thomas Grey. He died in 1622, and was buried in Rotherhithe in east London.

There were 102 passengers on board the *Mayflower* on her voyage to America – seventy-four men and twenty-eight women. There were also at least two dogs. One baby was born during the trip, named Oceanus Hopkins. Another, Peregrine (meaning wanderer) White, was born on the *Mayflower* on 20 November, once she had reached America, before the building of the settlement at Plymouth. Five passengers died on the *Mayflower* either before it reached America or before Plymouth had been established. William Butten was the first, dying at sea just three days before the coast of New England was sighted.

Mary Allerton Cushman, who died at Plymouth on 28 November 1699 at the age of eighty-three, was the last surviving passenger of the *Mayflower*.

six

GLIMPSES OF THE
SEVENTEENTH CENTURY

As one would expect, perhaps, our information about Billericay in the seventeenth century is fragmentary. We can capture a flavour of the place through a wide selection of formal records – court documents, wills and so on – but all this information is by definition partial. It is rare to glimpse day-to-day life directly; all we can do is make assumptions and draw conclusions from hints that appear, often incidentally. We can glimpse the social make-up of the town, for example, by looking at the occupations of those brought before the courts. Bequests in wills can tell us a lot about the wealthier classes' standard of living. Putting more than a little flesh on the bones is difficult, however; so much would be guesswork that it is possibly more helpful to describe some snapshots that have survived, and to view them in the context of a small market town that must have been like dozens of others: little affected by the world outside, with established modes of life continuing for decades – and longer – with few dramatic changes, just a gradual evolution. Here, then, are some of those snapshots.

In 1581 Great Burstead manorial court had set a property qualification for the keeping of greyhounds: no inhabitant of the manor could do this unless he was taxed for lands at 40s a year or £5 for goods by the subsidy, upon pain of forfeiting 20s. In about 1605 a local glover fell foul of this law, the Quarter Sessions describing him as 'a poor man not fit for that course of life'.

In 1605 an act of hooliganism occurred, when Robert Peacocke of Great Burstead had his chimney pulled down by a mob that gathered outside his house. One wonders why: sadly there are no other details.

Cases of witchcraft were still appearing before the courts in the seventeenth century. In January 1610 John Skafe of Great Burstead was before the Assizes for going to one Gressam, a soothsayer in London, about a lost horse and a man. In April 1616 John Scates, a weaver of Billericay, was before the Assizes on the evidence of Richard Tarling, a husbandman, for conjuring and practising with the devil for money.

In 1619 we find a case of someone who was arrested for drunkenness. The Michaelmas Quarter Session rolls for that year give the case of Robert Paprill, a box turner, who on the night of 15 September came from an alehouse in a drunken state. He was asked by Solomon Prowe, who was serving in the King's Watch (the town watch), to go along with him. Robert Paprill answered that he cared neither for the King's Majesty 'nor for such Jack an apes slaves as he was', and was thereupon arrested.

In 1639/40 there was a very interesting case concerning apprenticeships. While one often hears of wicked masters, there were also wicked apprentices. William Noone was a painter and barber from Billericay (an unusual combination of trades!). He petitioned the Quarter Sessions at Chelmsford in connection with Stephen Thorpe, who had been given to him at the age of nine by the parishioners of Hutton to be trained in the mysteries of painting and barbering. Noone had fed, clothed and tended Thorpe as though he was his own child, and had not abused him with hard usage or unreasonable correction. Thorpe, though, had shown himself to be rather wicked: he was involved in many robberies and broke more than twenty walls. He was sent to the house of correction in Chelmsford three times and to Colchester prison once, but to no avail. Noone therefore asked to be released of the boy, being supported in this by a number of citizens of Billericay and Great Burstead. The outcome is not known. Perhaps the parishioners of Hutton gave Thorpe to Noone as he was already a problem in their parish, and they wanted to be shot of him.

The market in Billericay was regularly a cause of problems in the seventeenth century. To quote an example mentioned by Harry Richman in *Billericay and its High Street*: at the Quarter Sessions at Chelmsford for 12 July 1651 John Stock of Billericay was charged with buying a load of butter before the opening of the market at ten o'clock on the morning of 24 June.

Following the Dissolution of the Monasteries in the previous century,

Burghstead Lodge dates back to the seventeenth century but was rebuilt a hundred years later. (Author)

responsibility for the maintenance of the impotent poor had passed from monasteries to parishes, and various poor relief acts were passed in that century. The administrative body in a parish was the vestry, which dealt with ecclesiastical and secular affairs, including poor relief. Sometimes poor relief was undertaken privately, as in 1664 when Roland and John Morton of the Weavers Company of London left some properties in Wellfield Lane (now Chapel Street), on the site of the Ritz Cinema, for the benefit of the poor weavers of Billericay.

Mention is often made of a connection between Billericay and the notorious eighteenth-century highwayman Dick Turpin, who is best known for a fictional overnight 200-mile ride from London to York on his horse Black Bess, in order to establish an alibi for a crime committed earlier that day. (This was first popularised by the Victorian novelist William Harrison Ainsworth – a century after Turpin's execution in 1739.) It was not Turpin, however, but another highwayman, named William (or John) Nevison, who made this epic ride rather earlier, in May 1676. Nevison was a highwayman on the Chatham road who, following a robbery at Gad's Hill in Kent at 4am, rode to York in fifteen hours – quite a feat considering he had to cross the Thames by ferry at Gravesend. The route he took would have taken him through Billericay. Arriving at 7pm, he spoke to York's mayor – entering into a wager with him at a bowling green. Though arrested for the crime, Nevison was acquitted when the mayor gave evidence; the jury considered it impossible to do the journey from Kent to York in a day. Knowing he could not be tried for the same crime twice, Nevison later revealed how he had achieved the feat to Charles II, who nicknamed him Swift Nick, on the basis that the devil, Old Nick, could not have ridden faster. Arrested for subsequent crimes, Nevison was executed at York Castle in March 1684. In 1836 the crack London to Thurso mail coach took twenty-one hours to reach York from London, over good roads compared with those that Swift Nick travelled. By 1841 it was possible to go from London to York by railway in just over ten hours.

Although we know that schools existed in Billericay in the sixteenth century, we have few details of them. In 1685 the Rev. Francis Bayley, rector of North Benfleet, left land in his will to the annual value of £35 to maintain a free school in the town; it became Billericay Grammar School. Ten poor children born in Great Burstead were to be taught freely by a master in the room at the market-place. In 1692 the Deed of Admission on the court rolls stated 'that the Trustees and their successors shall, out of the rents and profits of the

Nos 85 and 87 High Street were originally one house, which dated from the seventeenth century. (Basildon Heritage)

premises, pay to their Schoolmaster or Schoolmasters appointed by them to teach gratis ten poor scholars born in the parish of Great Burstead such stipend as they shall think fit'. Vacancies were to be filled as they arose 'so long as the schoolhouse over the market-place may be made use for the purpose'. Power was also granted to the trustees to fit up another convenient place in Billericay if the schoolhouse was converted to other uses. At a court held for the manor of Laindon on 13 April 1692, Samuel Bayley (son of Francis?) surrendered Laindon Watchhouse and 30 acres of land to the use of the Rev. Joseph Bedle, vicar, the successive vicars, four other trustees and himself for this purpose. The income arising from this property was to be used for the maintenance of the school. As well as catering for poor children, the school also served children whose parents were able to pay for their education. Only ten children of poor parents had free schooling.

An article in the *Essex Review* by E.P. Dickin details the availability of accommodation for guests and stabling for horses in 1686. This information is taken from War Office records that were compiled between 1686 and 1756, as part of the preparations for war or invasion. We find that Billericay's inns and alehouses had beds for fifty-four guests and stabling for 110 horses.

It is not known if there was any form of public transport from Billericay. An article in the *Essex Review* quotes a work written in 1637 that mentions the 'waines' (large open farm wagons) going from Stock to London every Wednesday. It is possible that they went via Billericay, but this is not proven.

Church House is a seventeenth-century building with eighteenth- or nineteenth-century extensions. (Basildon Heritage)

As regards roads, there is mention of the need for a bridge on the road from Ingatestone to Billericay at the court leet for Stock on 14 April 1658. The precise location is not known. It might have been to cross Stock Brook, which didn't have a bridge until 1925, or Buttsbury Bridge. The state of the roads into Billericay is also not known. The responsibility for road maintenance was in the hands of the parishes: under the Highways Act of 1555 every person who held a ploughland (an area of land roughly equivalent to a hide), and everyone else who owned a plough team, had to provide 'one wain or cart furnished after the custom of the country … and also two able men of the same' for four days a year. Every other householder, cottager and labourer who was physically able and was not a servant hired by the year had either to do four days' labour or send 'one sufficient labourer in his stead'. Under legislation passsed by Queen Elizabeth I the figure of four days was increased to six. Naturally this was rather unpopular, particularly in parishes where the vast majority of the traffic on the roads came from travellers passing through.

During the seventeenth century there were plagues, the most famous being the Great Plague of 1665. According to the Great Burstead parish records for that year, 'when there dyed in London of all diseases more 100,000 there dyed none in this parish for the spell of 12 weeks together'.

From the mid- to late 1660s we find evidence of the issue of local coins or tokens. For many years there was a shortage of small change, which was particularly difficult for the poor and shopkeepers, so tradesmen started to issue their own coins to solve the problem. These tokens, or pledges for money, were not legal currency but were used as such, although they could only be used at the shop of the issuer: a token issued by the butcher could not be used at the baker's. A number of people in Billericay are known to have issued tokens, and some have survived. Joseph Fishpoole, probably a wool dealer, had a woolpack and packing staff on his halfpenny of 1669; Miles Hackluitt had three tobacco pipes on his halfpenny of 1666; Edward Rhett had a sugar loaf on his farthing; Abraham Thresher, the landlord of the Red Lion, had three fleur-de-lis on his halfpenny; and Samuel Wayte, who occupied the Kiln House at the back of the Crown Inn, had a fleur-de-lis on his farthing. The making of tokens was made illegal in 1672, following the issue of farthings and halfpennies by the Royal Mint, and so they disappeared from circulation.

Other places in the vicinity of Billericay in which tokens are known to have been issued are Stock, Ingatestone, Brentwood, Rayleigh, Rochford and Chelmsford.

The reverse of Miles Hackluitt's halfpenny.
(Basildon Heritage)

seven

QUEEN ANNE TO NAPOLEON

In 1700 Billericay was still a minor centre of weaving, but by the end of the century there were no weavers at all in the town. It is not recorded when the last gave up their trade. The reason for the general decline of the Essex weaving industry was its dependency on a single type of cloth, for which there was a limited market in Spain, Portugal and Latin America; the market was thus rather vulnerable when war made communications difficult. Essex weavers were reluctant to adapt for other markets, and this was what ultimately caused the end of the Essex weaving industry.

In 1700 Billericay was still very much a market town. In an article in the *Essex Review* about the market in the days of Queen Anne, Felix Hull provides a lot of information. From the clerk of the market's accounts for 1700 we discover the stallage fees: butchers 6d a day, pedlars, cutlers, lacemen, shoemakers and toysmen 4d a day, gingerbreadmen, glassmen and orangesmen 3d or 4d a day, fishmen 3d a day, 'gardinors' (market gardeners), glovers, 'woostedmen' (worsted cloth sellers) and stockingmen 2d a day. For any 'strange-comers' a stall was 4d a day. Carts were charged 4d a day, wagons 6d a day. An edge toolman was charged 16s per annum and one Coules, a basketmaker, 40s per annum. The market house chamber was let at 40s per annum to a maltster named Thompson.

During June 1703 eleven butchers attended the market; on 15 June five were from Stock – John and Joseph Argent, John Clark, John Adam and Mr Goodbody. We find that certain trades attended the market regularly: butchers, market gardeners, glovers, shoemakers and a laceman were the most frequent; cutlers, pedlars and the orangeman less so; the glassman, the woostedman, the fishman and the stockingman only attended very rarely. Even the size of the market varied. For example, on 22 June 1703 there were twenty stallholders, but on 19 December 1705 only three. There was still a market cross at this time, for in 1707 3s 6d was paid for whiting and glue for it.

There were also permanent shops by this time. According to Arthur Brown in *Essex at Work 1700–1815*, in the period 1770 to 1775 there were fifteen shops in Great Burstead, of which eight were general shops, four were butchers, two were bakers and one was an ironmonger.

Of the non-conformist religions in Billericay, one of the strongest groups was the Congregationalists. In 1702 the former barn in Wellfield Lane (now Chapel Street) that was used by them for worship was described as a 'tenement formerly a barn and now known by the name of Meeting House'. The building was held in the name of Jeremiah Gunns; he was a woolstapler by trade and was the group's elder or deacon. The Congregationalists were not the only non-conformists in Billericay, as in 1704 there is known to have been a Quaker Meeting House.

As mentioned in the previous chapter, the administration of poor relief was in the hands of the parish vestries. The officials responsible were the Overseers of the Poor, but in some places special committees of the parish vestry ran the workhouse. Great Burstead was one of those places. In 1719 the overseers

borrowed a bond of £50 for the erecting of a workhouse, on the Laindon road. This was early for the construction of a parish workhouse, as their provision was not formalised until the General Workhouse Act 1723, which empowered parishes or groups of smaller parishes to build workhouses. In his book on Essex workhouses John Drury speculates that the Laindon road building was a house owned by the parish in which the poor were accommodated, rather than a formal workhouse with a workhouse master. The government's survey of workhouses in 1777 recorded that Great Burstead's workhouse had accommodation for up to

Billericay from Chapman and André's map of 1777. (Phillimore)

forty inmates, but Drury suggests that this was not on the same location as the 1719 building. If he is correct in this surmise, it is not known when the workhouse mentioned in the 1777 survey was built.

One way of helping people in need was through the friendly society. These developed from the premise that a group of people who contributed to a mutual fund could receive benefits at a time of need. In 1793 they were required by law to register with the Quarter Sessions. It is known that there were four friendly societies in Billericay. Artisans (craftsmen or skilled manual workers) were more likely to join than labourers: besides needing the protection, they were better able to afford the weekly fees. These could be as much as a twentieth of a labourer's weekly wage.

Another form of help, for those who could afford it, was brought about by the development of the medical profession. During the eighteenth century the number of doctors practising in Essex increased, and it is known that in 1790 there were four doctors practising in Billericay.

It was in 1724 that the first archaeological finds were made in Billericay, albeit by accident. According to J.A. Sparvel-Bayley in his article on Roman Billericay in the *Archaeological Journal*, volume 36 (1879), the first finds were made in November 1724 by a person who was digging for gravel in a field near Billericay. Having dug down 3ft, he came across a large quantity of earthen vessels of different kinds and colours. There was also what appeared to be an oven of hard dark clay, and several Roman coins were found.

In 1725 seventeen members of the Congregationalists acquired a lease of ninety-nine years on the property at the back of the High Street for a small rent. This was to be used as a meeting house for public worship for 'the Church Society or Congregation of Protestant Dissenters'. The old meeting house was pulled down, and a single-storey brick and tile rectangular structure was erected in its place. The church had something of a chequered history, as in 1741 the minister Robert Glass left to join the Church of England. His successor was Philip Davies. In 1749 the trustees of the church acquired the freehold of the land on which the meeting house stood.

As mentioned earlier, Richard 'Dick' Turpin (1705–39), the highwayman, is associated with Billericay – and was active in Essex from about 1730 to 1737. On one occasion he is supposed to have ridden his horse up the staircase at The Crown and jumped out of the window at the top to escape his pursuers. His ghost is reputed to haunt the Stock Road between Cromwell Avenue and Hill House Drive.

Crescent House dates from the mid-eighteenth century. (Author)

The entrance to Crescent House from the road. (Author)

These cottages in Norsey Road date from the eighteenth century. (Author)

Up until the beginning of the twentieth century, in Billericay as in a lot of other places, there was no fire brigade in the sense that we understand it. Fire prevention was in the hands of various fire insurance companies who maintained their own brigades according to the insurable values in any particular area. Unfortunately it is not known where they kept their fire engines. These companies put a plaque known as a fire mark on any properties they insured, often including the policy number. We know from Billericay of fire marks that existed for the Royal Exchange, Accident, Essex and Suffolk, Liverpool and London Globe, Norwich Union, Phoenix Fire, Royal and Sun Insurance. A Sun Insurance fire mark is now in the Cater Museum. In the event of a fire, only the fire brigade of the insurance company that insured the property affected would put out the fire. In Billericay, however, it appears that there was some co-operation between the various fire insurance companies. One notable fire occurred on 22 March 1742. It began at a house adjoining the chapel and consumed the house and the greater part of the chapel. The chapel was repaired.

By this time communications were improving, with the rise of stagecoach services. In 1755 the Maldon Stage Fly was started, running thrice weekly from Maldon to London via Danbury, Great Baddow, Stock, Billericay and Shenfield. When Billericay and Rochford became starting points for stagecoach services, the Maldon Fly was diverted via Chelmsford. In 1761 Rochford had a stagecoach service, which ran thrice weekly to Shenfield. By 1785 it was running daily. In 1776 Billericay got its own stagecoach service, and by 1794 this was also running daily.

As well as passenger services there were goods services. While some wagons conveyed commercial goods alone, such as those that took chalk from the Tilbury area to Billericay, there were also stage wagons that carried both goods and passengers. The people who operated these were called carriers, and they operated from the seventeenth century until the second quarter of the twentieth century. By 1800 there are known to have been three carriers who operated from Billericay to London. They tended to carry the poorest travellers who could afford to pay a fare, and they often travelled by devious country lanes to get the custom from out-of-the-way villages. At the other end of the scale were post chariots, which were coaches owned by inns and could be hired privately. In September 1769 Elizabeth Hirst of the Crown was advertising one, as was Abraham Thresher of the Red Lion.

With improved communications came increased mobility. Londoners began to move to Essex – which allowed them to travel easily to London when necessary but to live in better surroundings – and Billericay was one of the places they moved to. But it wasn't only people from London; there were also immigrants from Suffolk, no doubt attracted by the nearness of London. There were also people travelling in the opposite direction, leaving Essex for London; this was heaviest from south Essex. Under the Settlement Act of 1697 poor people could move to a new parish provided they took a settlement certificate with them – which protected them from being removed to the parish to which they 'belonged' if they survived on wages alone. If they applied for poor relief, however, they could still be returned 'home'. A quarter of those sent back to Billericay for lack of a settlement certificate had been trying to settle in London.

During the eighteenth century there were two post mills in Billericay, working as a pair and standing on Bell Hill – one to the east and one to the west of the road to Wickford. The eastern mill had been there since the sixteenth century, and is shown on Warburton, Bland and Smyth's map of about 1724; the western mill does not appear until Chapman and André's map of 1777. According to Kenneth G. Farries in *Essex Windmills, Millers and Millwrights*, documentary references to both mills are fragmentary. Billericay's miller in the latter part of the eighteenth century was Thomas Wood, who was something of a celebrity. Known as 'the Abstemious Miller' or 'the Ghastly Miller' of Billericay, he is probably the most intimately described of all Essex millers – although he was much more. A thoughtful man, in the days when horses were often ill treated he was concerned that they weren't overloaded or overworked. He was also something of a botanist, cultivating auriculas and holding open days at the mill to display his plants, and was an Overseer of the Poor. Thomas was born in 1719 and died in 1783. His place of birth was the wooden cottage next to the mill on Bell Hill. As a miller his life was quite ordinary. He took a twenty-one-year lease of the mill from Lord Petre, commencing at Michaelmas 1758. Between then and 1765 he built the second mill. This is mentioned in a quit rent entry of 1765 (quit rent was a tax on freehold), which describes him as owner and occupier of Millfield and the new mill built in it. In 1777 he wrote a book called *The Miller's and Farmer's Guide*. However, his fame rests on something else. As Farries says, Wood was born of parents who were somewhat intemperate. On reaching his majority he took to eating fat meat three times daily, supplemented by large quantities of butter, cheese and liberal draughts of ale. By the age of forty-four his weight had reached enormous proportions, and he began to suffer from a series of maladies: lowness of spirit, gout, sleeplessness, rheumatism, headaches, vertigo, heartburn, constipation, diarrhoea, a constant thirst and a sense of suffocation. He also had two epileptic fits – but somehow continued to work. In 1764 an acquaintance of his, the Rev. Mr Powley of Nevenden, to whom he explained his plight, suggested that he should change his eating habits and recommended a book, *Discourses on a Sober and Temperate Life* by a Venetian nobleman named Luigi Cornaro (1467–1566). Wood took his advice and gradually reduced his consumption of ale and animal foods over several years, taking cold baths and exercising with dumb-bells. By 1767 he was eating a diet of little more than a pudding made from sea biscuits mixed with skimmed milk. His health improved. When his cure came to the attention of the College of Physicians, a paper by Sir George Baker was published, based on information supplied by Dr Pugh of Chelmsford and Wood himself. His cause of death on 21 May 1783 was inflammation of the bowels; he was sixty-three years old. Wood had two children, a son Thomas and a daughter Elizabeth, named after his wife. When he died his estate passed to his son; his wife thereafter received £30 annually in equal quarterly payments; and his daughter received a lump sum of £800. In 1792 his son Thomas insured the new windmill of timber construction near his dwelling house for £240 and his utensils and stock for £130. He also insured the contents of the old mill for £130 and a separate dressing house for £100.

Cricket developed quite early in Billericay. There is a record of a match that was played in 1761 between Essex and Kent in the field behind the Crown inn. On 26 August 1771 a match was played at the same place between the gentlemen of Temple Mills and eleven picked men of Essex for a prize of £20. The Temple Mills men won by three wickets.

There were other pursuits. On Shrove Tuesday 1777 a 'cocking match' (a cock fight) was held at the White Hart between the gentlemen of the Rochford Hundred and a gentleman of Brentwood for 5gns a battle. Dinner was at 1pm, according to the advertisement in the *Chelmsford and Colchester Chronicle*.

From contemporary newspaper reports it is known that smuggling was carried on in the Billericay area. Unlike today, it was almost seen as a patriotic duty to be involved in some way, and all strata of society were affected. Kipling's poem 'The Smuggler's Song' aptly describes the prevailing attitude of the time: it says that the trade provided brandy for the parson and baccy for the clerk. The *Public Ledger* of 12 August 1765 reported that a seizure of French goods worth a considerable amount was made by revenue officers at a farmer's house near Billericay. The *London Evening Post* of 23 August 1766 reported that two horseloads of high priced tea were seized by revenue officers in a barn near

The White Hart, *c.*1900. (Basildon Heritage)

Billericay after a tip-off. The *Public Advertiser* of 14 March 1767 reported that on 12 March a valuable seizure of Indian goods was made by two customs officers in a farmhouse near Billericay. There were more reports in 1768 of smugglers being apprehended. The *Public Advertiser* of 14 February that year reported that on 11 February two horseloads of smuggled tea were seized in a barn near Billericay; the *Westminster Journal* of 20 February reported what might have been the same offence but dated it to 18 February. The *London Evening Post* of 7 January 1772 reported that some tea smugglers had been apprehended near Billericay by the excise men. The smugglers put up a fight, beat back the excise men and headed off towards London.

The eighteenth century saw the birth of the agricultural revolution. While this was not as dramatic as the industrial revolution it was still a revolution, as it began to alter agriculture beyond all recognition with the introduction of new methods and new machines. The campaigner for agricultural improvements Arthur Young was an occasional visitor to Billericay. In 1767 he toured southern England in six weeks, coming to Billericay from Chelmsford. He commented that between the two places the country was very rich, woody and pleasant with an abundance of 'exceeding fine landscapes' over extensive valleys. The husbandry was not equal to that north of Chelmsford. Young also commented on the type of manure that was used here. After talking about the state of the road from Tilbury to Billericay and of the chalk wagons that he met, he added: 'chalk being the principal manure they use about Billericay which they fetch in waggons from Grays, and costs them in general 5½d or 6d a bushel: they seldom use it alone, but mix it with turf, fresh dung and farm yard dung ... All this manure is sometimes spread at the expense of £10 an acre.' The nearer the coast Young approached, the more he found agriculture was for the London market than for crops to be consumed locally. Grazing to finish beef for the London market was almost a traditional form of agriculture near Billericay. Young also noted that from Billericay towards Tilbury the size of the farms was prodigious; rents of £700 to £1,000 a year were not uncommon – and a Mr Finch of Billericay rented his farm for £1,300 a year. In 1771 in his *Farmer's Tour Through the East of England*, Arthur Young wrote of Mark Duckett of Billericay: 'that ingenious agricultural mechanic, Mr Mark Duckett, whose implements have afforded more benefit to agriculturalists than to himself'. Duckett had made improved ploughs, hoes and drills, which helped local farmers because the soil around Billericay was 'strong', as Young subsequently described it in his *General View of the Agriculture in the County* of *Essex* (1807), thus needing large and powerful harrows. Duckett's patron in his work was Colonel Montague Burgoyne of Mark Hall, near Harlow.

Returning to Billericay town, there is an article in the *Chelmsford and Colchester Chronicle* for 29 January 1768 that sheds light, perhaps, on etiquette of the time – and also indicates that some people lived much longer in the eighteenth century than we would possibly realise. The previous Thursday John Ball, a tailor aged fifty, married an eighty-four-year-old widow, Mrs Heath. Mrs Heath was described as a wealthy and discreet gentlewoman, who to avoid the 'indecency' of marrying too soon after the death of her husband, had postponed her second wedding until the day in question.

Then there was scandal. The same newspaper of 3 January 1770 records that John Wilson and Edward Newman ran away from Billericay and left their families a charge to the parish. John Wilson was described as about 5ft 4in tall, with his own hair, a cast in his eye and much pitted with smallpox. When he disappeared he was wearing a dark coat with black horn buttons, a waistcoat striped with red and white, leather or fustian breeches and a round hat with a buckle in it. Edward Newman was described as a short man who was very cross-eyed. It was supposed that they were somewhere in the Rochford Hundred. The *Chronicle* said that whoever gave the officers of Billericay information that led to their apprehension would be reasonably rewarded; and that if the two gentlemen returned immediately to their families and properly provided for them they would be forgiven. The outcome of this is not known.

As ever, there were problems with disreputable inns and alehouses. At a Chelmsford Quarter Sessions in 1784 a witness said that he had stayed at the White Hart until 10pm and then gone on to the White Lyon (*sic*), where he had remained until 1am. Another witness said that he had remained there until 2am. It is no wonder that there was a demand for the tightening up of regulations governing alehouses, which was carried out by the Reformation of Manners in 1787. In enforcing a royal proclamation, the magistrates proposed a number of measures to control and reduce the number of alehouses: these included not granting a licence to a house that was not already licensed, unless another nearby alehouse had had its licence suppressed within the previous twelve months, and not granting a new licence to an alehouse keeper unless his behaviour was vouched for by four reputable and substantial householders, or the vicar, or the majority of churchwardens and parish overseers. In addition to this the parish constables were ordered to be more vigilant in the

A view of the windmill in its dilapidated state, *c.*1914. (Basildon Heritage)

Barnsley House and Foxcroft are both eighteenth-century buildings. (Basildon Heritage)

execution of their duties, in particular preventing drinking on a Sunday – the Lord's Day, when any pleasure was seen as inappropriate. Even before 1787 the magistrates restricted licences and required good order at inns. We know there were closures in Great Burstead, which of course included Billericay – but some later reopened.

Some of the bad behaviour at inns and beer houses was recorded in the newspapers. For example, in October 1772 the *Chelmsford and Colchester Chronicle* included a notice of apology by John Chapman, previously servant of Simon Raven, the innkeeper of the White Lion, for propagating a report to the prejudice of his late master. Another apology appeared in the *Chronicle* (and the *Ipswich Journal*) in October 1768: Robert Bundock of Ramsden Bellhouse apologised for having raised a scandalous and false report, and abusing Elizabeth Hirst, the innkeeper of the Crown. Mrs Hirst had prosecuted Bundock, and when he asked her pardon she stopped the proceedings against him. Oddly, in 1769/70 Mrs Hirst was mentioned as the innkeeper of the Red Lion, to which she seems to have temporarily transferred. Her stay at the Red Lion was short, and by the end of 1770 she was back at the Crown.

It was usual at this time for the local press to be used to alert creditors and debtors to someone's death. An example appeared in the *Chronicle* on 15 April 1760: anyone who was indebted to the late Benjamin Johnson of Billericay, a matter and tallow chandler, was required to pay their debts to his administrator at the deceased's house within two months, or they would be sued. Anyone with just demands was requested to send an account to the same place. A week later Daniel Davan, who had been Johnson's apprentice, put an announcement in the *Chronicle* to the effect that he had taken over the business. On 19 August that same year the *Chronicle* advertised that the White Lion was to let, with the whole of its stock in trade and household furniture to be taken by appointment. By this time it was occupied, with its brewhouse, stables, other outbuildings and a large cherry orchard, by John Davan – not Daniel. It is recorded that John died in January 1771.

The state of the roads around Billericay in the eighteenth century was poor. The worst was from Billericay to Tilbury. Arthur Young's famous description dates from 1769:

> Of all the roads that ever disgraced this kingdom in the wry ages of barbarism none ever equalled that from Billericay to the 'King's Head' at Tilbury. It is for near 12 miles so narrow that a mouse cannot pass by any carriage … the ruts of an incredible

depth ... the trees everywhere overgrow the road so that it is totally impervious to the sun except at a few places, and to add to all the infamous circumstances which occur to plague a traveller, I must not forget eternally meeting with chalk wagons, themselves frequently stuck fast until a collection of them are in the same situation that twenty or thirty horses may be tacked to draw them out one by one ... After this description, will you – can you believe me when I tell you, that a turnpike was much solicited by some gentlemen, to lead from Chelmsford to the ferry at Tilbury fort, but opposed by the bruins of this country – whose horses are worried to death bringing chalk through those vile roads. I do not imagine that the country produces such an instance of detestable stupidity; yet in this tract are found farmers who cultivate above £1,000 a year.

Although not mentioned by Young, the road from Billericay to Chelmsford was difficult in that not only were there the hills at Stock to be contended with, but also there was no bridge over Stock Brook at the foot of the hill leading up to Stock from Billericay.

Responsibility for the maintenance of roads lay with individual parishes, and consequently the state of repair varied considerably throughout the country. One solution was the turnpike system, in which gates were set up across the roads and tolls were collected before travellers could pass. The money collected paid for maintenance. Originally turnpikes were controlled by magistrates, but later they were taken over by groups of local businessmen. The first turnpike gate in Essex was set up in 1696 on the Great Essex Road at Mountnessing. This later became part of the Essex Turnpike Trust, an organisation that controlled most of the turnpiked roads in the county, including the one from Shenfield to Billericay and Rayleigh, with branches to Rochford and Leigh – which was turnpiked in 1747. The road from Shenfield to London was controlled by the Middlesex and Essex Turnpike Trust. The road to Chelmsford from Billericay was not turnpiked, but tollbooths are known to have existed in Stock Road. In 1765 there was a proposal for turnpiking the road from Billericay to Tilbury, but nothing came of this until 1793 – when the road was granted to the Hadleigh Turnpike Trust. By 1820 it had been abandoned. The Essex Turnpike Trust survived rather longer into the railway age.

During the eighteenth century there was a state lottery. The *Morning Chronicle* of 29 November 1774 reported that three people of Billericay bought a ticket in it. One of them sold his share the next day for an advance of 5s. When the lottery was drawn the ticket won a prize of £10, much to his

Stock Road and the former toll house. (Basildon Heritage)

mortification! Other people were unlucky in Billericay too. The *Chelmsford and Colchester Chronicle* of 10 October 1777 reported that a gentleman's servant from Hornchurch who was sent to Billericay fair to buy cattle was decoyed by some cardsharpers into the White Hart. In the ensuing game he lost £80, as well as a £20 banknote, which he believed the cardsharpers picked from his pocket. They immediately took off towards London.

War or the threat of it was a common occurrence during the eighteenth century. The militia often camped at Billericay or took cantonments (temporary billets) in the town. Sometimes the soldiers caused problems. They were not always from Essex. For example, according to the *General Evening Post* of 22 February 1783, a company of Radnorshire militia quartered in the town mutinied and behaved in a 'most outrageous manner' to several inhabitants, who intervened to prevent the men 'destroying' their commanding officer. Parties from different regiments the next day prevented further mischief, and took more than twenty of the offenders into custody. Apparently the Radnorshire men had seen a magpie in a shop, and were determined to take it back to Wales with them – so they broke the shop window. According to the

Morning Herald and Daily Advertiser of 25 February, the soldiers were to be tried by court martial and if guilty would be sentenced to death. The result of the trial is not known.

The Church of England chapel was becoming dilapidated as the end of the century approached. In 1775 a Brief was published to authorise the collection of £1,650 in England, Berwick on Tweed, Flint, Denbigh and Radnor in Wales, from house to house in Essex, Middlesex, Hertfordshire, Suffolk and other counties, to pay for the chapel's rebuilding. It was described as 'a very ancient building' that was 'very decayed', and it was stated that even if it was repaired it would be too small for all the parishioners to attend services. Perhaps repairs after the fire of 1742 had not been carried out well, or perhaps the chapel was just becoming too small for its congregation. Whatever the situation, as it was separate from the mother church of Great Burstead no tax could be raised for repairs. The estimated cost of rebuilding was £1,650 13s 7d, and this money was eventually raised. When the rebuilding was finally completed in 1784 only the tower of the old church remained.

Arthur Young, who wrote about the abominable state of the road from Billericay to Tilbury and the state of agriculture in the area, was widely regarded as the leading writer on agriculture in his day. He was born in 1741 in Bradfield Combust in Suffolk, the second son of the Rev. Arthur Young, who was the chaplain to the Speaker of the House of Commons Arthur Onslow, and was educated at Lavenham Grammar School. Young unsuccessfully tried his hand at being a merchant, and when that failed he attempted to become an army officer. This also came to nothing, so his mother put him in charge of her family's estate at Bradfield, although he had very little knowledge of farming. Here he carried out a number of agricultural experiments and engaged in his interest in writing, publishing *The Farmer's Letters* in 1767. Though Young's experiments were on the whole unsuccessful he acquired a detailed knowledge of agriculture.

In 1765 Arthur Young married Martha Allen, the sister-in-law of the music historian Charles Burney. The marriage was a rather tempestuous one. By this time he had already started a series of journeys through England and Wales; his accounts of them were published in three books that appeared between 1768 and 1770: *A Six Weeks' Tour through the Southern Counties of England and Wales*, *A Six Months' Tour through the North of England* and *The Farmer's Tour through the East of England*. Young claimed that they contained the only extant information on the rental, produce and stock of England that was based on actual examination. These books were well received. In total he wrote twenty-five books and pamphlets on agriculture, including *General View of the Agriculture in the County of Essex* (1807), and fifteen books on political economy. He also visited Ireland and France, and wrote books on his findings there.

In 1793 Young was appointed secretary to the Board of Agriculture, and in this capacity he gave very valuable assistance in the collection and preparation of surveys of the state of agriculture in the English counties. However, as a result of developing cataracts his eyesight failed, and in 1811 he had an operation that proved unsuccessful; ultimately he lost his sight.

Young lived on until 1820. At his death he left an autobiography in manuscript form, which was not published until 1898.

eight

UNDER ARMS

The Napoleonic Wars lasted from 1792 to 1815 – a series of wars declared against Napoleon's French Empire by opposing coalitions. This was when larger armies were used for the first time, and when the concept of arming a nation became popular among military innovators. In Britain, for example, the army increased in size from approximately 40,000 in 1793 to a peak of 250,000 in 1813. This indicates, perhaps, the immense impact that the wars had on Britain as a whole.

On 20 April 1792 France declared war on Austria, following this by declaring war on Britain and Holland on 1 February 1793. At first there were no major battles, and little effect on the populace. Rumours that the French were contemplating an invasion of England were countered by the English blockading the Channel ports – but by 1796 it was clear that rumours had become reality: France was in a position to genuinely threaten England with invasion. In 1797 a report was drawn up by Major Thomas Vincent Reynolds of the 30th Regiment of Foot, explaining what should be done in the event of an invasion. A summary of this report is included in the accompanying text box.

According to an article written by Eva E. Barrett in the *Essex Review* in 1913, almost all the male population in Essex was under some form of military training, either in the militia, the volunteer army corps, the guides or pioneers (who opened roads for the army or closed them to the enemy), or as guerrillas (to harass and annoy the enemy). Robert Edward, 9th Lord Petre, raised a company of volunteers from the districts of Ingatestone, Brentwood and Billericay, and their banners were still hanging in Ingatestone church in 1848. According to J.L. Cranmer-Byng in 'Essex Prepares for Invasion 1796–1805', which appeared in the *Essex Review* in 1952, 'Lord Petre in a letter to the Lord Lieutenant, intimated that he intended to form his Tenants and other respectable house-keepers into a Military Association, and to collect a body of Pioneers and offer the same to H.M. Service free of all expense to the Government.' He produced two plans: to form a voluntary association of Pioneers at Thorndon Hall and another for Ingatestone, Mountnessing, Fryerning and Margaretting; and to form a volunteer company.

The local nobility, gentry and farmers were asked to sign statements showing how many wagons, horses and carts could be placed at the disposal of the country for immediate use and with two days' provisions. The form that was sent out asked for the following information: the names of owners, the number of wagons with four or more horses, the number of carts with three horses, the number of carts with two horses, the number of drivers and the number of conductors. Routes were drawn up to allow livestock that was kept near the coast to be driven inland. Billericay is mentioned in connection with the route from the Rochford Hundred in the Returns for 1801: 'Rochford Hundred – Between the Crouch (including Wallasea, Foulness and the other islands) and Hadley Ray. The stock of this Hundred will cross the London Road between Moutnessing Street and Margaretting Street and proceed to Ongar and Bishop's Stortford. The principal roads leading from the Thames to the London Road, particularly the one through Billericay, must not be driven upon except in the necessary crossings, which must be done as quick as possible.'

The local millers and bakers had to send in details of how much flour and bread they could supply. According to J.L. Cranmer-Byng the millers were all asked to fill in a form which was worded as follows:

WE the undersigned MILLERS of the ... of ... in the County of ... having taken into Consideration a Plan recommended to our Attention by ... Lord Lieutenant and Custo Rotulorum of the County aforesaid,

For ensuring a regular supply of Bread to His Majesty's Forces in the ... District, during the Continuance of the Present War, in case it should become necessary to assemble large Bodies of Men, in one or more given Points, for the Purpose of opposing an Enemy,

Do hereby declare our Approbation of the same. And we do most readily and faithfully promise and engage to deliver such Quantities of ready-made Flour as we may happen to have in Hand, over and above the immediate wants of our Customers; and also to prepare and deliver such Quantities of dry, clean and sweet Flour, made of good marketable ENGLISH Wheat out of which the Bran shall have been taken by means of a Twelve Shilling seamed Cloth, and as expressed opposite to our respective Names, whenever we shall be required to do so, the whole in the manner, and upon the Terms and Conditions specified in the Plan herein-before mentioned.

And we do hereby appoint … residing at … for the Purposes expressed in the 5th Article of the said Plan.

Do hereby declare our Approbation of the same. And we do most readily and faithfully promise and engage to bake and deliver such quantities of good, whole-some and well baked Bread, in Loaves of Three Pounds as our Stock of Flour in Hand at the Time may enable us to furnish over and above the ordinary con-sumption of our Customers; and also to bake and deliver such quantities of good, wholesome and well baked Bread, in Loaves of Three Pounds as expressed oppo-site to our respective Names out of such Flour as may be delivered to us for that Purpose, whenever we shall be required to do so, the whole in the manner, and upon the Terms and Conditions specified in the Plan herein-before mentioned.

And we do hereby appoint … residing at … for the Purposes expressed in the 12th Article of the said Plan.

They were asked their name, the name and state of their water- or windmill, the number of sacks of flour weighing 280lb that they could furnish every twenty-four hours, and whether the miller would provide the wheat or not.

Bakers were asked to fill in a similar form, 'for ensuring a regular supply of Bread to His Majesty's Forces in the Eastern District, during the Continuance of the Present War, in case it should become necessary to assemble large Bodies of Men, in one or more given Points, for the Purpose of opposing an Enemy'. They were asked their name, the number of loaves they could supply every twenty-four hours, normally and in an emergency, the kind of fuel their ovens needed and how much per day, and how abundant that fuel was.

Plans were drawn up for the evacuation of civilians. Signal stations to communicate news of an invasion were established at high points in the county, of which Laindon Hills, Cowe Green and Rettendon were the nearest to Billericay. Cowe Green had a signal hut, while Rettendon's signal station was on the church tower. On Laindon Hills and at Cowe Green piles of straw faggots and tar barrels were erected, to be lit in the event of an invasion. To ensure that a false alarm did not happen it was made illegal to light bonfires. According to documents in the National Archives, if there was an invasion it was intended that Billericay would be the rendezvous point of the Rangers, Labourers and Reserves from the district between the Crouch and Purfleet Magazine. If the French captured Colchester it was proposed to abandon Chelmsford, which was the northern hub of London's defences.

During the war troops were billeted in Billericay's alehouses and inns. The army paid an allowance of 5d per soldier to each innkeeper or publican towards the cost of board and lodging; the government also paid 11d per soldier. Several inns had soldiers' rooms, exclusively reserved for them – but friction was caused when rooms that could have been used for travellers were taken by troops, causing a loss of trade

Although the Rising Sun building probably dates from the eighteenth century it did not become an inn until 1810. In 1822 coaches left here daily for London and Southend. (Author)

and custom. In addition, the High Street was used for regimental parades, which were colourful but no doubt disruptive. These two factors resulted in several petitions to the authorities. Troops could be rather rowdy, and whether through thoughtlessness, high spirits or deliberate unpleasantness they created problems. During one period of six months, when 10,773 troops and 1,727 horses had been billeted in the town, damage that valued £894 6s 0d was caused, according to a complaint made by Billericay innkeepers to the government. The government sent an assessor to investigate the damage, and he felt that a payment of £50 to the innkeepers was suitable recompense. The offer was accepted. Despite this episode, the innkeepers were still happy for the troops to stop in the town: in 1799 they petitioned the War Office to allow Billericay to continue to be the military halt between Chelmsford and the Tilbury Ferry.

We do not know all the regiments that were billeted in Billericay. Some troops from the North Lincolnshire militia spent the winter of 1793–4 in the town, the West Essex regiment of the militia was billeted there in 1795 and the Havering Yeomanry at the time of the Golden Jubilee of King George III in 1810. Between 1804 and 1807 barracks in a plot of land bounded by Sun Street and Wellfield Lane were erected for troops; they housed up to 276 men, ordinary soldiers in smaller buildings and officers in a larger one. These barracks remained in use for about ten years, probably until just after the end of the Napoleonic Wars in 1815. *Jackson's Oxford Journal* of 29 June 1816 records that

Billericay infantry barracks (among others) were to be reduced. They were put up for sale in 1817, but were not surrendered by the barrack-master, Osborn Markham, to the new owner, William Rolph, until 3 June 1819.

As the wars continued, normal life in Billericay was mostly unaffected. There were, of course, unexpected events. In 1798 the Congregational church minister Richard Fry was sacked for embracing Unitarian principles. Unitarians did not accept the principle of the Trinity; they believed that God was one person. Part of the congregation left with Fry, and they built the New Meeting House for him in Wellfield Lane. Unfortunately Fry felt that he was not propagating Unitarianism as successfully as he might, and shortly afterwards he left the town. Some of his followers returned to the Congregational church, but the New Meeting House continued for a time to be served by Unitarian preachers. Things settled down in 1800 when the Rev. Richard Thornton arrived in Billericay from Yorkshire. He was pastor for forty-one years and a very active minister, who was responsible for establishing Congregational churches in Stock, Ingatestone and Wickford.

It was during the Napoleonic Wars that Billericay's Congregational minister was moved to open Sunday schools by the sight of people enjoying themselves on a Sunday. As Arthur Brown writes in *Prosperity and Poverty in Rural Essex 1700–1815*, he became aware of 'the most disgusting scenes of wickedness: some spending the wages of the week, while cursing and quarrelling … others moving in the fields on excursions of sinful pleasure, and crowds of ragged boys and girls vying with each other in exploits of wantonness and mischief'.

In 1806 we find a mention of the Grammar School. There is a somewhat obscure sentence in a decision of the Trustees: 'so long as the present school house in Billericay hired for the occasion shall continue to be made use of as a school for the purpose aforesaid (the market-place, with the room over it having been some time pulled down, and the Chapel having been erected on the site thereof). In case the present school house shall not continue to be hired or used for the purpose of a school, the Trustees to fix up some other place.' Harry Richman writes in *Billericay and its High Street* that the removal of the Grammar School from the market house happened in 1806, but the document perhaps suggests that the market house was pulled down when the chapel was rebuilt and expanded in the latter part of the eighteenth century.

There were also dame schools, private educational establishments that charged a small fee. In 1807 Great Burstead had five, one with ten pupils, two with seven and two with six. Of these we only have information about Mrs and

Chapel Street and the Congregational church, *c.*1910. (Basildon Heritage)

Miss Cannell's Ladies Boarding Academy, which existed in 1790. They charged 10gns a year, including board, and taught English, writing, accounts, drawing, dancing and music.

By now there were local banks in Billericay. Before the passing of the Bank Charter Act of 1844 all banks could issue their own notes, and some bank notes issued in the town are known to have survived. A £1 note of 1808 from Crisp and Butler has Britannia standing with a shield and a lion at her feet, and the monogram C&B. Another £1 note dated 1814 was issued by Fincham, Barrett, Fincham and Fincham: the design is a sheaf of corn. The Billericay Bank also existed, as we know from a scandal that involved it: forged notes allegedly issued by the bank were passed in London. It eventually crashed, paying a dividend of only 10s in the £1.

In November 1810 the Golden Jubilee of George III was celebrated. According to the *Chelmsford Chronicle*, Billericay and Great Burstead celebrated with the ringing of church bells and a church service in St Mary Magdalen. After that the inhabitants, preceded by the men of the Havering Yeomanry, paraded through the town singing, and at intervals a band played 'God Save the King'. The poor of the town sat down to dinner opposite the town inns, their meal consisting of beef, plum pudding and strong ale. Apparently they were very well behaved! The *Chronicle* also records that the more 'respectable inhabitants' sat down to an excellent dinner at the Crown Inn.

In 1811 there appeared the first proposal for a railway in the vicinity of Billericay. This was for an 'iron railway' to run from Islington to Wallasea Island with a branch to Mucking. The main line would have passed through Little Burstead. Had it been built it would have used horses as its motive power, and

The old vicarage dates back to at least 1815. (Author)

would have been similar to the Surrey Iron Railway. This opened in 1804, and ran from Wandsworth to Croydon; with the Croydon, Merstham and Godstone Railway it later reached Reigate and Godstone.

It was during the Napoleonic Wars that Arthur Young made another visit to Essex, which he recounted in his *General View of the Agriculture of the County of Essex*, published in 1807:

> From Billericay, by Ramsden and Downham to Wickford, the general feature is strong and heavy; but above Wickford there is a vale of lighter land, and very good loam it is, one or two feet deep; the wheat stubbles there brighter and indicated much better crops than I had travelled with of late.
>
> The basis of the soil at Billericay is a reddish gravel full of blue round pebbles: at Stock the soil is lighter and there the subsoil is white sand and gravel; though gravel is so prevalent at Billericay, yet the loam mixed and superincumbent is so stiff that there are very few turnips to be seen in the country and there ought to be none …
>
> Around Billericay they have in use very large and powerful harrows for their strong land, which they call ox harrows, heavier and more effective than the common crab harrow of the county. The name is proof that oxen were in use but before the memory of man.

According to Young the average rent of the country around Billericay was 15s. Tithes at Billericay were 5s an acre.

MAJOR VINCENT REYNOLDS'S 1797 REPORT

In 1797, when invasion fears were at their height, Major Thomas Vincent Reynolds of the 30th Regiment was commissioned to report on how best to cope with an invasion by Napoleonic forces.

According to Major Reynolds the body of the hill on which Billericay stood took the shape of a bow. The least accessible side of the hill was on the south-east, and in the event of an invasion this would have been the side most exposed to the enemy. The front was secured by a number of points of land that projected from the body of the hill, flanking and commanding the surrounding area. The soil on the hills was of stiff clay except near the town and towards the western summit, where it was of hard gravel. The approaches to Billericay, except by the turnpike road from Rayleigh and the road from Laindon Hills, were generally unsuitable for artillery, while 'the skirts and assents' were 'very thickly enclosed', for the most part laid out as small pastures with strong fences around them. To the north-east of Billericay was Norsey Wood and some other smaller woods, which strengthened the left flank. The hill on the east side of the turnpike road commanded the best look-out in the district: it was possible to see not only places in Essex such as the military campground at Danbury, Burnham on Crouch and Rayleigh church, but also as far as Kent. The major went on to mention open grounds near Billericay, i.e. Ramsden Common, Ramsden Heath, Stock Common and Galleywood Common, which he felt were unsuitable for occupation by troops because of their soil. He proposed the encampment of a large body of troops nearer to Billericay instead.

nine

IN DECLINE

I n the last decade of the reign of King George III the introduction of threshing machines caused farm labourers, who saw mechanisation as a threat to their jobs, to try to destroy them. In October 1819 the *Essex Chronicle* reported that on the 14th of that month a fire had broken out in the stackyard of Mr R. Browning of Little Blunts, off Perry Street, which threatened the destruction of the whole premises. Fortunately fire engines arrived in time from Billericay and Ingatestone, and only a large wheat stack and a straw stack were destroyed. Two labourers named Clark and English were later apprehended and arrested on the suspicion of setting fire to the property; they were gaoled.

Despite this and similar disturbances, it is worth noting that a sense of community must have been growing during the nineteenth century. One way in which this was expressed was a growth in competitive sport, with the people of Billericay organising themselves into teams and competing against their neighbours. In 1816 we find mention of cricket matches, when Billericay beat Rayleigh twice and Benfleet once. A return match against Benfleet was called off – as rain stopped play.

In 1823–4 there were many 'academies' in Billericay (a 'Ladies Day', a 'Ladies Boarding', a 'Children's Day', 'a Ladies Boarding and Day', and a 'Gents Boarding Academy'), as well as the Burstead House Academy for Congregational church children; this was latterly known as Price's Academy because Mr J.H. Price was the master. There was a British School (also for Congregational church children, and used on Sundays as the Congregational church Sunday school), a National School (for Church of England children, built in 1839), a free school and, of course, the Grammar School. Until the passing of W.E. Foster's Act of 1870 education was in the hands of private individuals, charities and religious bodies, which meant there was a great proliferation of educational provision.

As the century progressed Billericay's transport links with its hinterland and London continued to improve, with the road network becoming ever more important and other forms of transport growing up as well. According to *Pigot's Directory* for 1822–3 stagecoaches departed from the Crown Inn to London via Brentwood and Romford at 7am and 11am, to Southend via Rayleigh and Rochford at 3pm and 5pm, and to Chelmsford every Friday at 11am. From the Sun Inn there was a coach to London every morning at 7am and to Southend every afternoon at 5pm. There were also carriers' vans operating: Thos Fitch's went to London every Thursday at 5pm; John Pease's went to London every Monday at 5pm, while John Hammond's went to London every Sunday, Tuesday and Thursday afternoons. Every Saturday at 7am Thos Rochford, Pease and Fitch's van went to Southend. By 1832–3 the timetables had changed. The Despatch coach from Southend called at the Crown at 11am every morning on its way to London and every evening at 5.30pm on its way to Southend. Thorogood's coach stopped at the (Three) Horse Shoes every morning, at 8am in the summer and 9am in the winter, on its way from Southend to London, and every evening at 5.45pm on its way back to Southend. By this time an 'omnibus' went to Chelmsford from the Bull every afternoon at 4.30pm. Of the carriers only John Pease is mentioned: his van left his house for London every Monday and Thursday at 4pm and for Rochford every Wednesday and Saturday at 10am. There is no mention of coaches to Billericay from Chelmsford, but Livermore Isaac's cart departed from the White Hart in Chelmsford to Billericay every Tuesday.

In 1825 there was a proposal for a canal from the River Crouch near Battlesbridge to Purfleet, with a branch from Battlesbridge via Rettendon to Billericay – but only the plans for the branch canal were deposited with the county Clerk of the Peace. This canal to Billericay, had it been built, would have been 7⅓ miles in length, and from Battlesbridge to a basin near the lower end of the meadows in Chantry Farm would have risen 181ft. Boats would have entered the canal at sea level by an entrance lock, and then almost immediately would have risen through a further five locks. After that there would have been seven intermediate locks, and the final rise of 100ft to the terminal basin at Billericay would have required sixteen locks. This gives a total of twenty-nine locks in the canal's 7⅓ miles, or an average of about one every quarter of a mile. By comparison the Chelmer and Blackwater Navigation had thirteen locks in 13⅞ miles, just under one every mile, and a fall of about 75ft. In the 1821 census Chelmsford was a prosperous market town with a population of 4,649 people, whereas Great Burstead and Billericay had 1,861 people. While Chelmsford obviously benefited from its canal, there is no guarantee that a small town like Billericay would have done likewise.

There is a bit of a mystery about Billericay's market house in the early part of the nineteenth century. A plan of Joseph Fishpoole's lands dated 1681 shows the market house at the junction of the High Street and Wellfield Lane, on the site of the war memorial. According to Harry Richman in *Billericay and its High Street* this market house closed in 1830, and a new building with the Grammar School and the Assembly Room was erected at what is now 94 High Street. However, as mentioned above, in *Billericay and its High Street* Harry Richman says that the Grammar School moved from the market house in 1806, quoting a

Billericay from *Pigot's Directory for Essex* for 1822–3. (Author's collection)

document that says 'the market-place, with the room over it having been some time pulled down, and the Chapel having been erected on the site thereof'; but Wynford Grant suggests that the old market house was pulled down when the church was rebuilt. In his history of St Mary Magdalen's church (1959), which information is repeated by Sylvia Kent in her history of the church (2007), G.S. Amos states that this was completed five years after a collection was authorised for this task in 1775 – in other words in 1780. The dates don't appear to match up – but credence is given to 1830 by a photograph of a foundation brick from the building that clearly shows this date; the image is reproduced in Ted Wright's *Billericay Times* (1999). To add confusion, *Pigot's Directory* for 1822–3 says that 'There is a handsome modern built market house', a statement repeated in the 1823–5 edition. The market house is not mentioned at all in *Pigot's* for 1832–3 or 1839. A drawing of the church dated 1830 does not show the market house in front of it at the junction with Wellfield Lane, just trees. Old maps are not always the best sources, though. So what happened between 1806 and 1830? Was a 'modern built market house' provided in 1806, only to be replaced in 1830? If so, where was it?

Well developed as a market town, Billericay was also expanding in other ways. We know that there was a brewery in the town – the Billericay Brewery Estate. This originally belonged to the Crown Inn and was an integral part of that building – a fact that is mentioned in a notification of the sale of the Brewery Estate and Inn, which took place on 29 January 1830. In *The Times* of 18 May 1822, quoting from the *Chelmsford Chronicle*, there is an item regarding the price of beer in Billericay. Brewers in Chelmsford, Great Baddow, Writtle and Billericay had resolved to drop the price of their beer, so that publicans could sell mild beer at 4½d a pot and 'old beer' at 5½d a pot.

The town's growing importance is also indicated by the establishment of a post office; this was in existence by 1832, and William Curtis was the postmaster. The post arrived by mail cart from Ingatestone every afternoon at 1pm and was dispatched every morning at 8am. Nearby Ingatestone was one of the stopping places of the London to Norwich mail coach.

Early in the nineteenth century, with the rise of silk weaving, Billericay became a minor centre of the industry. It does not seem to have stayed long: although there is a mention of it in *Pigot's Directory* for 1832–3, when John H. Machu is described as a silk manufacturer and thrower and it is implied to be one of the main industries of the town, there is no reference to it in *Pigot's* for 1839.

Administratively there were changes in the locality, as there were nationally. In 1834, following the passing of the Poor Law Amendment Act, the parishes of Basildon, North Benfleet, South Benfleet, Bowers Gifford, Brentwood, Great Burstead, Little Burstead, Childerditch, Downham, Dunton, East Horndon, West Horndon, Hutton, Ingrave, Laindon, Mountessing, Nevendon, Pitsea, Ramsden Bellhouse, Ramsden Crays, Shenfield, Thundersley, Vange, Little Warley, South Weald and Wickford were grouped together to form the Billericay Poor Law Union. (As Billericay was historically part of Great Burstead it was not mentioned.) Great Burstead, Brentwood, East Horndon, Pitsea, Thundersley and South Weald had their own workhouses at the time of the Act: Great Burstead had two, both in Billericay, one known as Great Burstead workhouse, the other as Billericay workhouse; one of them was the former barracks. The Act required that the Poor Law should be administered by three commissioners, with inspection of the workhouses delegated to assistant commissioners, to whom Boards of Guardians were responsible for day-to-day management of parochial poor relief, although the parishes themselves continued to levy the poor rate. The provision of outdoor relief was greatly reduced by the Act, and conditions in the workhouses were made as unpleasant as possible, so that they were perceived as a last resort. Each parish in the Union submitted one name to be on the Board of Guardians except for Brentwood, Great Burstead and South Weald, which were allowed two.

The Town Hall, formerly the market house, was built in 1830. This photograph was taken in the 1950s. (Basildon Heritage)

Following the creation of the new Union, Brentwood, East Horndon and South Weald workhouses were closed and their inmates were transferred to either Great Burstead or Thundersley. It was April 1836 before thoughts were given to making alterations and additions to the existing workhouses so that they could accommodate up to 250 inmates each. Advertisements were placed inviting architects to come up with plans. In June 1836 the Guardians decided to follow the Poor Law Commissioners' guidelines and to allocate Great Burstead workhouse to women, Thundersley to children and the new Billericay workhouse to men. In November 1836 Thundersley workhouse was closed and the inmates were transferred to the old Great Burstead workhouse. By April 1839 thoughts turned to building a completely new workhouse in Billericay, and a committee was formed to inspect potential new sites. Six were selected, and eventually the one in Norsey Road was bought from a Mr Butler for 350gns. The new building was completed in 1840 and the inmates from the other two existing workhouses were transferred there. The architect was George Gilbert Scott.

Church life continued, with the Congregationalists under the ministry of the Rev. John Thornton being particularly successful. In 1814 their old meeting house had become too small and was enlarged, but a few years later it became obvious that a new chapel was needed. In the spring of 1836 a meeting was held to form the Weekly Subscription Society, the purpose of which was to raise funds to this end. Joseph Radford was appointed treasurer and George Rolph was appointed secretary. Ten women were responsible for collecting subscriptions. The Chelmsford architect Mr T. Fenton was asked to inspect the existing building, and gave the opinion that while it could be rebuilt for £300 the end result would hardly be substantial. In his view £600 would pay for a new building, which would be far more commodious, safe and modern. The next meeting, on 10 May 1836, agreed this course of action. On 17 May the Rev. Mr Thornton was asked to take over as fund treasurer, and it was decided that two thirds of the required sum was to be collected before work commenced. Within a short time £520 had been raised. It had been intended to erect the new chapel on the site of the old building, but as the subscribers became more confident of their success they decided to look for a larger site. George Rolph, who owned some land in Wellfield Lane near the main London to Southend road, offered part of it with a frontage of 80ft for £60, and this was accepted. During the building of the new chapel Roman remains were found. The last service in the old meeting house was held on 28 April 1838 and from

The former Billericay workhouse's Elizabethan-style buildings. (Basildon Heritage)

May to October services were held in the market house, for a fee of 7s a week paid out of weekly donations collected at services. The new chapel opened in October 1838 – but sadly Mr Thornton did not live for long, dying on 2 May 1841. The old chapel was demolished, the site being carefully cleared so as not to interfere with the tombs and graves that clustered in the yard outside the building's walls. The ground on which the building had stood became part of the graveyard, and was used until 1913.

Major events continued to draw the community together. As an example, for the coronation of Queen Victoria in 1838 dinner was provided for children from Billericay's various schools. They were addressed by the rector of Dunton, as the vicar of Great Burstead was unable to attend.

As the nation entered the Victorian period there were many signs that long-established modes of existence were changing. Looking back, we can see that this was the turning point, when the foundations of modern life were laid. An example of this is the creation of the Essex Police Force in 1840, following the Police Act of 1839. The new force took over the roles of the King's (or Queen's) Watch and the parish constables. Billericay was part of the force's Brentwood division, and initially there were two constables stationed in the town, answerable to the divisional superintendent. As there was no police station in Billericay, they would either have worked from their lodgings or from a building temporarily leased to the county. We do not know the first two constables' names or where they worked from.

In the latter part of 1841 or the early part of 1842 a small iron foundry was established in the former Great Burstead workhouse in the Laindon Road to make agricultural implements, iron pots and so on. The owner was Mr Offwood Bendall, who also had a foundry at Manningtree. The *Essex Herald* of 8 November 1842 reported that on the previous Tuesday evening (1 November) a number of gaslights had 'sent forth their brilliant rays' in Billericay from several shops and inns. The gas was supplied from Mr Bendall's works; he had erected the lights 'at his own expense and engaged to supply both public and private lights on reasonable terms'. Compared with candles and oil lamps, gaslight was a tremendous improvement. In 1851 Mr Bendall's premises and business were acquired by Job Jeffrey Salter.

As Billericay grew in size and local significance, so the townspeople gained a greater sense of importance and community. For example, the congregation at St Mary Magdalen increasingly felt that their church should have its own parish – so that religious life could be managed locally. In 1844 an application

The Congregational church and rectory. (Basildon Heritage)

The Rose Hall was formerly the Congregational school and is now the local Royal British Legion branch headquarters. (Author)

was made to the Bishop of London, asking him to use his influence to obtain a permanent endowment from the Ecclesiastical Commission for the maintenance of the chapel chaplain and the assignment of a district under his charge. As the chapel was under private patronage, according to the commission's constitution no such endowment could be given, so the patrons surrendered their rights to the Bishop of London, with the proviso that the application be granted and that they retained through their wardens control of finances and services. 'We surrender, but not completely' seems to have been the order of the day. As a result of this application, on 3 September 1844 authority was given by an Order in Council for marriages, baptisms, churchings and burials, with all fees being assigned to the minister. The parish registers of Billericay commence from that date; earlier they were at Great Burstead. St Mary Magdalen in Billericay was first styled as such by an Order in Council dated 26 April 1845, when the patronage was transferred. The first incumbent was the Rev. J.K. Bailey, the resident chaplain. It was not until 12 April 1860, however, that the new parish of Billericay formally came into existence and the annual election of churchwardens began.

The newly appointed vicar made an impact straight away. The population of Billericay in 1841 was 1,284 and the stated seating of the church was 386 pew rents – 30 per cent of the population. The vicar proposed to add 186 free seats for adults and 70 for children, bringing the total to 486. In addition repairs to the fabric of the church were necessary. The cost of all this was £209 for the seats, £230 for the repairs and £20 for the architect's fees – a total of £459. Mr Bailey applied to the Incorporated Church Society of Westminster for a grant, and they gave £100; the balance was raised by subscription. On 29 January 1846, nine months after the original application, the work was completed. The altar was moved from the north apse to the east apse, and new seats were installed. Brian D. Gennings wrote in 2007 that it is 'interesting to note the distinction between adults seats and children's seats. The picture springs to mind of a compound where children can be penned in, while adults attend divine service.'

Reforms to national life continued. In 1835 Rowland Hill published a pamphlet that led to the establishment of the Uniform Penny Post throughout Britain on 10 January 1840; for the first time the safe, speedy and cheap delivery of letters was possible. From 6 May postage prepaid with the first postage stamp, known as the Penny Black. In 1845 William Curtis was still Billericay's postmaster, his post office standing on the site of the car park in

St Mary's Avenue that was opened in 1961. Letters arrived from Rochford at 8pm and from London at 1pm, and were delivered at 7am from 25 March to 29 September and at 8am for the remainder of the year. The post box closed at 7pm.

In 1839 the Eastern Counties Railway was opened from London to Romford, reaching Brentwood in 1840 and Colchester in 1843 – but stagecoach services continued – and to some extent were integrated with the newer mode of transport. *Kelly's Directory* for 1845 lists stagecoaches 'per railway' from the Crown at 8.30am, 9.30am and 2.30pm, returning from Shoreditch station at 4.45pm. Whether these coaches merely connected

Billericay from Kelly's Post Office Directory for 1845. (Author's collection)

with the trains at Brentwood or were placed on flat wagons on the trains is not clear. A coach went from Billericay to Rayleigh, Rochford and Southend every afternoon at Sunday at 4.30pm; there was also a coach from Southend to London that passed through Billericay, calling at the Sun at 9.30am on Mondays and 11.30am on Tuesdays to Saturdays, returning at 5.30pm Monday to Saturday. The long-established carrier wagons were still vital to many, being cheaper than the new-fangled railways: Thomas and William Pease's wagon went to London every Monday, Thursday and Friday and returned every Wednesday and Saturday. On Wednesday and Saturday their wagon went to Rayleigh, Rochford and Southend, returning every Monday, Thursday and Friday. Painter's van went to Chelmsford at 9am every Monday, Wednesday and Friday and returned the same day at 6pm.

In 1845 came the first proposals for steam-operated railways directly serving Billericay. The first for which there is a record was the Metropolitan Railway's Junction Railway of 1845, which would have run from Reigate to West Tilbury, around the outside of London in a clockwise direction. In Essex it would have gone from Chelmsford through Widford, Margaretting, Fryerning, Ingatestone, Buttsbury, Mountnessing, Great Burstead, Laindon, Little Burstead, Bulphan, Dunton, Laindon Hills, Horndon-on-the-Hill, Orsett, Chadwell and West Tilbury. Nothing came of this. In the same year there was the first proposal for a railway to Southend that would serve Billericay: it was the London and Southend Railway and Dock Company, which was to run from Shenfield east of Brentwood to Southend, via Billericay, Wickford, Rayleigh, Rochford and Prittlewell – the ancestor of today's railway from Shenfield to Southend. The railway was to terminate on the foreshore at the low water mark, where the construction of a dock was proposed. Apparently the scheme failed because the board of the Eastern Counties Railway told the promoters that they could not support the scheme. However, between 1848 and 1850 a station was opened on the site of today's Shenfield station.

Religion still had the potential to create neighbourhood tensions. The town was scandalised in 1847 when Edward Dewhirst, who had been the preacher at the Independent Chapel, renounced the principles of dissent and decided to conform to the Church of England. On joining the Established Church, he decided to seek holy orders.

What of crime? Records seem to indicate that Billericay was similar to many similar towns in Essex and beyond. Violence was minimal (often drink-fuelled when it occurred at all), and theft was never very serious. In November 1850, though, there occurred the most violent murder recorded in the area.

THE MURDER OF PC ROBERT BAMBOROUGH, NOVEMBER 1850

Robert Bamborough had just arrested a poacher, William Wood, at the pond just below the Crown Hotel. Wood wasn't coming quietly, though, and took the policeman's truncheon, striking him and knocking him down. He then took hold of the constable and threw him into the pond, whereupon he took his victim's head, opened his mouth and put mud in it. Pushing the policeman under water, and holding his mouth open, Wood then stood on him – before departing along the lane opposite. A little girl aged eleven who saw the attack take place from the front window of a nearby house said that it was a few minutes before anyone went to help the victim. Although a passer-by named Mr Thompson lifted Robert Bamborough's head out of the mud, and the policeman was taken away for treatment within a quarter of an hour, he was so badly injured that he died a few days later in excruciating agony. At his trial at Chelmsford in March 1851 Wood was convicted of manslaughter, and sentenced to transportation to Australia for life.

ten

BILLERICAY RESURGENT

By 1855 stagecoaches had disappeared and the only public road transport left was provided by the carriers. Thomas Painter went to Chelmsford on Mondays, Wednesdays and Fridays at 9am, Denton went to London on Mondays and Thursdays at 6pm, and Pease went to London on Mondays, Thursdays and Fridays at 6am, to Rochford on Mondays, Wednesdays, Thursdays and Saturdays at 8am, to Romford at 5am on Wednesdays, and to Southend on Wednesdays and Saturdays at 8am.

The great period of 'Railway Mania' was the 1840s – peaking in 1846, when there were 272 Acts of Parliament to set up new railway companies. This speculative frenzy eventually ran its course – and around a third of the lines that were authorised were never built. The resultant financial crash had an impact on individuals and on the economy of the country as a whole. Despite this salutary experience, economic upturns in the following decades saw smaller booms in railway construction, but these never reached the same scale – because of limited government control, more cautious investors and because there were fewer opportunities for new lines. Events in Essex illustrate what was happening elsewhere: complex networks of investment, ownership and finance, together with a combination of new lines and proposals for new lines that were never completed. In the 1850s the London, Tilbury and Southend Railway (LTSR) was promoted. This ran, as one would expect, from London to Southend via Tilbury. Although a separate company, it was initially owned by the London and Blackwall and Eastern Counties railways and leased by the contractors Peto, Brassey and Betts; there were a few independent shareholders. The Eastern Counties Railway (ECR) provided the engines, carriages and wagons and operated the services, as agents to the lessees. In 1862 the lessees of the LTSR, trying to escape from the lease on which they were making a loss, obtained an Act of Parliament that constituted the LTSR as a separate company. At last the shareholders had a partial say in the future direction of the railway.

In 1856, the year the LTSR reached Southend, Peto, Brassey and Betts backed a railway from Pitsea to Colchester via Maldon, with a branch from Cold Norton to Burnham on Crouch – the Tilbury, Maldon and Colchester Railway. They were also the contractors for the East Suffolk Railway, which was ultimately intended to run from Lowestoft and Yarmouth to join an authorised but not yet constructed Eastern Union Railway line from Ipswich to Woodbridge, at Woodbridge. The proposal was to obtain running powers over the Eastern Union Railway from Colchester to Woodbridge, and thus have a line from London to Lowestoft and Yarmouth independent of the ECR. The ECR responded with a blocking move – proposing lines from Shenfield to Pitsea via Great Burstead, Wickford, Rayleigh, Hockley and Rochford, Maldon to Pitsea, Maldon to the Chelmer Navigation Basin and Rayleigh to the River Crouch, near Burnham on Crouch. The Tilbury, Maldon and Colchester was abandoned at the end of May when Peto, Brassey and Betts and the ECR agreed that the latter would work the East Suffolk. Nothing further came of the ECR's proposed lines. In 1862 the ECR amalgamated with some other railways in the eastern counties to form the Great Eastern Railway (GER).

In 1864 there were more plans. The East Essex Railway was proposed, running from Shenfield via Billericay, Wickford, Woodham Ferrers, Cold Norton, North Fambridge, Althorne, Southminster and Tillingham to Bradwell. Nothing came of it. The South Essex Railway was another scheme: a line from Great Warley to Southminster, with a branch from Rettendon to Heybridge; the main line would have passed through Great Burstead. In 1866 an Act was passed that gave permission for a line from Rettendon to Pitsea – but the railway company was unable to raise sufficient funds to start construction.

In 1875 the LTSR acquired its own carriages and goods wagons, and in 1880 its own engines. At the beginning of the 1880s there were plans for the development of Tilbury Docks, and the LTSR could see that when this occurred there would be a lot more traffic on their line to London. However, the line from London to Southend via Tilbury was about 41 miles long, and not very direct, and there was a perceived need to shorten this route. There was a proposal to do this by building a link from Barking to Pitsea, and in 1882 an act authorising the construction of this new line was passed.

Having lost control of the LTSR, the GER wanted a line to Southend, and decided on the Shenfield–Billericay–Wickford–Rayleigh–Rochford route. In a speech that he made at the opening of the railway through Billericay to Wickford for passenger traffic, on 1 January 1889, Mr H.J. Emerson, a linen and woollen draper in the town, said that this was his doing. In 1882 he had concluded that only a railway would improve the town's prospects – and that he had written to this effect to the manager of the GER. The reply he received asked for his proposed route, which was from midway between Brentwood and Ingatestone, through Billericay, Ramsden Crays, Wickford, Rayleigh and Rochford to Southend. Emerson then forwarded his correspondence to the editor of the *Essex Chronicle*, who took up the matter. This account has been disputed. According to the *Essex Standard* and the surviving records of the Great Eastern Railway, the call from Billericay for a railway can be traced back to 1878, and the proposal for the line as it was built can be traced back

The poster that announced the meeting at which the proposal to build the railway was discussed. (Great Eastern Railway Society collection)

to 1880. Mr Emerson's name does not appear in these sources. The decision by the GER to build the Shenfield to Southend line with branches to Maldon and Southminster was taken at a meeting of the company special board on 24 October 1882, and confirmed by the full board on 7 November.

Meanwhile the LTSR couldn't avoid learning about the GER's proposals, and in opposition proposed a line from Pitsea to Southend, via North Benfleet, Rayleigh, Hockley, Rochford and Prittlewell. They also backed an independent Mid Essex Junction Railway from Ingatestone to Pitsea, via Mountnessing, Buttsbury, Great Burstead, Laindon and Basildon. This line would, of course, have served Billericay – via the Great Burstead station. At Billericay the railway would have crossed the Hutton to Wickford road to the south and east of the town, and would also have crossed the road going round the back of the north-western part of the town. On Tuesday 20 March 1883 a meeting was held in Billericay Town Hall to discuss the GER's proposals. Most of those who attended supported the railway company. Later in the year Parliament passed the GER's proposal for the line from Shenfield to Southend, together with lines from Wickford to Southminster and Woodham Ferrers to Maldon, and rejected the LTSR's proposal for a line from Pitsea to Southend.

Construction of the line started in June 1885. One gets the impression that the construction of the railway through Billericay and elsewhere attracted spectators. Certainly my maternal grandfather remembered being taken to see it, and saw a steam excavator in use. According to the contractors one man and one boy lost their lives building the 9-mile section of railway from Shenfield to Wickford. By the standards of the day this was reckoned to be light: the general rule was the loss of one man per mile.

The first part of the line to be opened was a new station at Shenfield, at the junction with the main line, on 1 January 1887. On 19 November 1888 the section of line from Shenfield to Wickford was opened to goods traffic. This had been delayed because of serious slips in several places – most seriously in the deep cutting on the Wickford side of Billericay station. The problem was overcome with the help of a substantial drainage system and elaborate retaining walls, which increased the cost of this section of line from the tendered price of £104,996 to £140,580. Despite all this extra work, the Board of Trade's inspecting officer was still concerned about slippage, and would not allow passenger trains to run. According to the *Essex Chronicle* of 23 November 1888, the first train, consisting of thirty-three trucks, laden with manure, coal and other goods, left Shenfield for Wickford at about 9am. The journey was accomplished without a hitch. On the engine were Mr Denning, the inspector of the goods department of the GER and other officials. The train returned from Wickford at about 11am.

The initial service was two trains a day from Shenfield, at 9am and 2.15pm, and from Wickford, at 11am and 6.30pm. On or just after 29 December 1888 there appeared a poster announcing the opening of the line to passenger traffic to Wickford on 1 January 1889, following a further inspection by the Board of Trade's inspector. The first train was the 7.37am from Wickford, which was late: it had run empty from Stratford (where the GER had its main engine shed and carriage sidings), and there had been fog. The passengers were two women and a policeman. The *East Anglian Daily Times* noted that the driver was a Mr Pollock and the guard a Mr Sparrow, while Mr G.C. Taverner was acting relieving stationmaster at Billericay, where the station boasted two platforms and a goods yard. A lot of people joined the train at Billericay for the journey to Shenfield, where the first train to Wickford was due to leave at 8.10am. The 10.15am train from Liverpool Street, which normally terminated at Brentwood, was run that morning as a special from Brentwood to Wickford. It conveyed the local MP, directors of the GER and the contractors' representatives.

The new line of railway from Shenfield to Wickford was opened for goods traffic on Monday. A train consisting of 33 trucks, some of which were laden with manure, coals, and other goods, left Shenfield about nine o'clock, and

proceeded to Wickford, returning from that place about eleven o'clock. Mr. Dissite, inspector of the goods department, and other officials, were on the engine, and the journey to and fro was accomplished without a hitch. It is proposed for the present to run two goods trains daily from Shenfield to Wickford and back. The trains will leave Shenfield at nine a.m. and 2.15 p.m., and Wickford at 11 a.m. and 6.30 p.m. It is expected that the line will be opened for passenger traffic in January next.

An extract from the *Essex Chronicle* recording the opening of the railway from Shenfield to Wickford for goods trains, November 1888. (*Essex Chronicle*)

At Billericay the Maldon town band played 'See the Conquering Hero Comes' as the train steamed into the station. Later it returned from Wickford, and there was a public luncheon in Billericay Town Hall at 1.30pm. It was at this event that Mr Emerson told of how the railway was his doing! The newly constructed Railway Hotel and the High Street were bedecked with flags.

Initially there were six passenger trains a day to and from Shenfield on Mondays to Saturdays. Of these five went to or came from Wickford, and one terminated and originated at Billericay. On Wednesdays, Fridays and Saturdays there was an additional train between Shenfield and Wickford. There were no Sunday trains.

On 1 June 1889 the line was extended to Southminster for goods trains. Passenger trains followed on 1 July. The July timetable said that the opening to Southend and Maldon was expected to take place in August (to catch summer traffic to Southend, presumably), at which point the service would be revised – but in fact the opening did not occur until October. On 1 October the lines from Wickford to Southend and Woodham Ferrers to Maldon were opened, with great celebrations in Southend.

According to Ken Butcher, writing in the *Great Eastern Journal*, the earliest known stationmaster at Billericay was Henry Hambleton, who was known to have been in post in 1890 – it is likely that he replaced Mr Taverner. Hambleton was succeeded in August 1902 by William Joseph Joslin, who in turn was succeeded in January 1905 by Horace Thomas Bassingthwaighte. He was in post until the end of September 1930 and was the town's longest-serving stationmaster.

The coming of the railway must have changed the pace of life in rural Essex. Improving transport links brought many benefits, including wider markets for manufactured goods – but this wasn't enough to save some old-established occupations. For example, Billericay was the last place in Essex where leather breeches and gloves were made. John H. Smith was the last person to carry out this trade, ceasing between 1859 (when he appears in the *Post Office Directory*) and 1863 (when he does not). Some new industries were encouraged, however. From 1858 until 1915 gravel was dug in Norsey Wood. There were two major periods: between 1858 and 1889, when there were diggings in the western part of the wood, and between 1895 to 1915, focused on the central area. In the course of the gravel excavation the workmen found a large amount of Iron Age pottery, Roman tiles, a potter's oven and a lead-smelting furnace. Sadly, because of the workmen's clumsiness, many of the artefacts were broken on discovery. As mentioned in Chapter Two, they also discovered a ditch and a cave that may have been connected with the Peasants' Revolt.

There were further archaeological discoveries elsewhere in the 1860s. A Mr Wood found a large number of urns containing burnt human bones at Ramsden Hall and also in the mill fields. A Mr Shaw recorded the discovery on the same site of a small British coin and Roman coins. In 1865 the Rev. E.L. Cutts opened tumuli in Norsey Wood, discovering bones, urns and coins. In about 1877 workmen digging a hole for the construction of a new gasometer came across a mass of broken Roman pottery. Mr J.A. Sparvel-Bayley hastened to

The passenger train service from *Bradshaw's Railway Guide,* November 1889. (Author's collection)

Billericay station platform, January 2008. (Author, courtesy of Greater Anglia)

the site and investigated. His account of his findings was published in an article in the *Essex Archaeological Transactions* in 1878. A few years later, in 1880, Mr Sparvel-Bayley carried out excavations in Norsey Wood, and discovered a large burial place with stones, tiles and broken pottery, and what were obviously burnt human remains.

In 1862 the market house was purchased by the Town Hall Company Ltd from George Shaw, into whose hands it had fallen. In the same year the first police station was established in the Town Hall; the officers based there were Inspector George Thomson, Sergeant Michael Keavan (or Keving) and Constable Finch. The police shared the building with the local magistrates' court, which had cells at the rear. In 1863 the Grammar School hired a room in the Town Hall for a twenty-one-year lease – a new lease on their existing school room. When the Grammar School closed in 1904 the entire Town Hall was taken over by the police.

After the passing of the Education Act of 1870 all facets of education were taken over by local authorities, in Billericay by the Great Burstead School Board. This was formed on 13 February 1873, and immediately a search began to find a plot of land on which to build a new school. A plot measuring just over

1½ acres was found in the Laindon Road and was purchased from the trustees of the late Thomas Richardson of Downham for £259. This money was loaned by the Public Works Commissioners, with repayment over fifty years. The architect for the new school was a local man, a Mr Cutts, and the building work was undertaken by Messrs Ruffell and Cross, who were also local. The new school was opened on 10 September 1878 by a local landowner, Major Thomas Spitty. While the new school was being built the School Board had used the British School as the girls' classroom (on Sundays it had continued to be used as the Congregational church Sunday school) and the Church of England's National School as the boys' classroom. With the passing of the Education Act of 1880, education became compulsory for all children aged between five and ten. At ten a child could leave school by obtaining a certificate – but only if his or her attendance was satisfactory. Primary education had to be paid for until 1891; secondary and further education in schools had to be paid for even after this. The school leaving age was raised to eleven in 1891 and twelve in 1899.

Sport continued to grow in importance as the Victorian era progressed. In 1875 Billericay Cricket Club was formed, until about 1900 playing its matches on Laindon Common. After this it moved to a field near the present Billericay School, and for two seasons before the First World War it played on a field behind the Catholic church in Laindon Road. Before the formation of an

Quilters, formerly Great Burstead Board School, opened in 1878. (Basildon Heritage)

official cricket club there was an unofficial Billericay Cricket XI, whose leader was Dr Frederick Carter. In 1880 Billericay Town Football Club was formed – the eleventh oldest football club in Essex. In 1890 it moved into the Romford and District League, competing in that league until 1914. A very different sport was fox hunting, whose association with Billericay goes back a long way. In 1869 the Essex Union Hunt built kennels at Great Burstead.

Once again we return to the effects of easier transport for the masses. About 25 miles from central London, Billericay was becoming a popular country destination – far enough from the city to be a change of air, but close enough to be within striking distance. The *Chelmsford Chronicle* for 5 August 1881 recorded that on the previous four Saturdays the town had been greatly enlivened by the presence of the employees of several London firms, who came to partake of the good things provided for them by Thomas Side of the Lion Inn. The previous Saturday there had been eight brakes each drawn by four horses, bringing nearly 200 men to Billericay. The party's entrance into the town was witnessed by hundreds of people with delight, but everything went wrong when the men went for a walk after dinner. They entered people's gardens, breaking and stealing from fruit trees, and picking flowers. One group went into the Reading Room and threw books about, threatening to 'break open the library'. Another group walked through the town with stinging nettles, drawing them across the face of anyone who happened to be in the way. After a few fights among themselves in the Brentwood Road, the men 'got clear away'. As the newspaper reports, Sergeant Aylett and Constable Day, though greatly provoked, 'showed an evenness of temper, a promptitude of action and a presence of mind worthy of all praise'.

As the century progressed, Billericay must have become a more pleasant place to live. Until sewers were built, what was delicately known as night soil was collected from properties and disposed of in a suitable place, primarily on wasteland. In 1884 sewage began to be treated with a solution called milk of lime, to make it less unpleasant. Some sewers were built in 1898, but because they discharged untreated sewage into ditches or watercourses they were not very satisfactory. In 1912 Billericay finally got a proper sewerage scheme, built jointly by Billericay Rural District Council and Brentwood Urban District Council; it cost £20,000. The scheme was proposed in late 1908/very early 1909, with an application by the two authorities to the Board of Local Government for permission to borrow money for it being made in late February 1909. The original estimate of the cost was £21,000. *The Times* of 26 October

High Street, with the hunt exercising, 1900s. (Basildon Heritage)

1912 reported that the new sewage works had been opened by Dr Thresh, the Medical Officer for Essex.

In 1909 the Southend Waterworks Company laid the first mains water supply in the town. Before that date water supply was mainly from private wells, except on clay soil where filtered rainwater, from tubs sunk on roadsides or watercourses and springs, was used.

Another major advance for the people of Billericay was brought about when the Isolation Hospital was built on the Mountnessing Road just off Perry Street in 1886. Also known as the Fever Hospital and Mayflower Hospital, it was used by patients with infectious diseases. In 1881 there were a hundred diphtheria cases in the town, of which ten were fatal; in 1885 there were fifty-two cases of smallpox, of which six were fatal. The hospital was a wooden building and unfortunately burned down in 1890, but it was quickly replaced, and in 1899 was enlarged, with proper drainage for the first time. The building was still inadequate, though, and in 1901 a field in Jackson's Lane, later Green Farm Lane, was purchased as the site of a tented isolation hospital.

Infrastructure continued to improve, with the formation in 1892 of the Billericay Gas Company. It was not very successful, however, and in 1897

The railway and The Crown from the station approach side of the railway bridge. (Basildon Heritage)

The railway bridge, with the workhouse in the background. (Basildon Heritage)

the company's property was sold to a business named Worthington Church. In 1913 it was sold again, this time to the Grays and Tilbury Gas Company. Shortly afterwards gas ceased to be made in Billericay, and thereafter it was supplied from Grays.

Towards the end of the nineteenth century local authorities started to take over the supervision of fire prevention. It is known that one George Bassom was the captain of Great Burstead Fire Brigade at the end of the nineteenth century. In about 1907–8 a fire station in Chapel Street was opened, and a horse-drawn manual fire engine was stationed in it.

No. 89 High Street, Lloyds Bank, dates from 1890. (Author)

Culturally the town was developing too. In 1886 the current Reading Rooms were built at 73 High Street. They had been founded in 1864 by Major Thomas Jenner Spitty, but detailed early history has been lost, including the location of the original Reading Room. A modest library was provided, together with a range of newspapers and periodicals. It was perhaps more of a social centre than one would assume: bagatelle was played there, and in 1900 a billiard table was installed – a second in 1908.

After the Roman Catholic Relief Act was passed in 1829, Catholics were free to fully participate in public life. In 1884 the first Roman Catholic mass since the time of the Reformation was held in Billericay at 108 High Street, the home of Mr and Mrs Cole, by Father William Cologan. Father Cologan was the parish priest of Stock, who shortly after his appointment in 1877 was given responsibility for the Roman Catholics in Billericay. Their number greatly increased during the building of the railway, when there was an influx of Irish navvies. They were accommodated in a wooden hut on the site of what later became the goods shed (demolished in the 1960s when the goods yard was closed) and is now part of the station car park. On Sundays mass was said in this hut, and other Catholics in the town had free access. Sometimes Father Cologan presided; sometimes a priest came from Romford on horseback. When the navvies left, the remaining Catholics naturally wanted to continue to have

The Reading Rooms, built in 1886. (Basildon Heritage)

regular masses said in Billericay. From 1888 to 1909 Father Cologan said mass at a variety of places: at the Temperance Hotel and in the Blue Room at 72 High Street, as well as at Mr and Mrs Cole's home. In 1909 Dr and Mrs Waldron took up residence at Norsey View in Western Road, and allowed Catholics to assemble there every fortnight for mass. In 1910 the Ursuline nuns took a lease of the large mansion at 129 High Street, and established a convent there until 1913. For the first time since the Reformation there was a resident priest in Billericay – Father William Donelan, who lodged in a house adjoining The Shambles. As soon as the nuns had left, along with Father Donelan, thoughts were given to establishing a permanent Catholic church in Billericay. The site found is still occupied by the church today. William Dunn of Lilystone Hall at Stock contributed half of the cost and the local Catholics the rest. Father Donelan was succeeded by Father Martin Brassil. The foundation stone of the new church was laid by Bishop Butt of Westminster on 21 November 1913, and the first portion of the church was opened and blessed by Bishop Butt on

8 September 1914. At this time the church was not complete, as it lacked a sacristy. Part of the south aisle was curtained off for the purpose.

In 1887 there were celebrations for Queen Victoria's Golden Jubilee, and churches were expected to hold a public service. While the Church of England did so, apparently Billericay's Congregationalists thought it undesirable. According to the *Essex Chronicle* the parish church was crowded. A hot dinner was provided for pensioners, there were athletic sports in the afternoon and then tea for children – after which their parents and friends were permitted to enjoy any food that remained. They were not the only ones who had a meal, as there was also a dinner for forty gentlemen in the Assembly Room. A firework display rounded off a full day of celebrations.

In about 1890 Billericay's brewery closed, the Crown Inn having shut shortly after 1859. One of the two windmills did not survive either. The west mill seems to have fallen into disuse by the end of the nineteenth century, and its superstructure was removed probably in about 1892. The east mill survived until the First World War and beyond, last working in about 1902. *Kelly's Post Office Directory* for 1902 does not mention a miller, but the 1908 edition lists Robert George Walker as the 'miller (steam)'. This suggests that after the mill fell into disuse Walker tried to revive it using steam power. The use of steam or other power sources was not uncommon in later years; for example, Stock Mill used a steam engine and later a petrol engine. There is no mention of a miller at Billericay in the 1914 edition of *Kelly's*, which suggests that Walker's revival was short lived.

By the end of the nineteenth century local government was becoming rather unwieldy, and between 1885 and 1894 a number of far-reaching reforms were implemented. The Local Government Act of 1888 saw the creation of the counties that would remain in existence until 1974, together with municipal and county borough councils. The London Government Act of 1889 saw the creation of metropolitan borough councils. The Local Government Act of 1894 brought urban and rural district councils into existence, as well as parish councils. Under the 1894 Act Billericay, while remaining part of the parish of Great Burstead, became part of the newly formed Billericay Rural District Council. Until 1899 Brentwood was also included, but in that year it became a separate UDC. It is not absolutely certain where the offices of Billericay RDC were situated – and in Kelly's Directory for 1908 and 1914 the address of the clerk was in Brentwood. According to Harry Richman in *Billericay and Its High Street*, in about 1914 the surveyor of the RDC occupied 108 High Street,

Billericay from *Murray's Handbook of the Eastern Counties*, 1892. (Archive CD Books Ireland)

and for a number of years this was the only council accommodation. Indeed, the council met at the workhouse on alternate Tuesdays: at 10.30am in 1908 and 10.15am in 1914.

Queen Victoria's Diamond Jubilee soon came round, in 1897, and the *Essex Chronicle* records that the houses and streets were well decorated. A new clock on the parish church was inaugurated by Mrs Spitty, and there was a bonfire in the High Street.

In 1898 there occurred a particularly sad case at Cray's Hill. On 5 February Miss Charlotte Kate Kenny Howard married Charles Emanuel Leppar Enkel. Two days after the wedding she complained of feeling unwell and took to her bed. A local doctor found her to be suffering from inflammation of the kidneys, which was believed to be the result of contracting a cold while selecting her trousseau in London. Her death took place on 11 November. She was buried in her bridal attire. It is not recorded whether Charlotte was treated at home or in the small infirmary of forty-four beds that was built for the sick in 1898, after extra land had been purchased adjacent to the workhouse. This was the beginning of Billericay Hospital.

Until the end of the 1870s agriculture hadn't done too badly in Essex; even the 1846 repeal of the Corn Laws (which had protected English agriculture) had not caused problems for county farmers. But from 1875 things went badly wrong. Cheap prairie-grown wheat arrived from America and Canada, while refrigerated meat arrived from South America, Australia and New Zealand. In 1878 the harvest was ruined by some of the worst weather imaginable. Rain day after day soaked corn sheaves, so they were sprouting before they could be carted for threshing. The winter of 1878–9 was so hard that farmers were drilling winter wheat in January, and the spring corn was sown in the worst possible conditions. When hay-time came rain filled the brooks, flooded the meadows and carried the haycocks away down the stream. The harvest of 1879 was long and protracted, and in many parts the yield was no more than three

Jubilee cottages in Norsey Road. (Author)

sacks of wheat or barley to the acre. A lot of farmers gave up: in the areas of the Poor Law unions of Billericay, Rochford and Maldon about 11,000 acres of land ceased to be cultivated in the 1880s, and they were still derelict at the beginning of the First World War in 1914. Lord Petre, the lord of the manor of a large part of Essex, advertised in Scotland for farmers to come and take over his land. And down they came – mostly from the south-west of Scotland – as enormous rent increases on Scottish farms were making life unsustainable, and Lord Petre was offering more favourable terms. Not only did the trains from the north bring the farmers and the families, but also their livestock and even their machinery. At one time Burns night was celebrated in Stock.

At the end of the nineteenth century Billericay began to change from a country town into a dormitory town. This process began when Lord Petre disposed of many of his holdings in the area, among them the manor of Buckwyns in Buttsbury and the area that became known as Queen's Park. Speculators moved in and drew up plans for large-scale intensive building, the proposed roads being named after members of the royal family. Nothing really happened, though, until after the end of the First World War.

The Jubilee clock on St Mary Magdalen church. (Author)

THIS CLOCK WAS ERECTED BY THE INHABITANTS OF BILLERICAY IN COMMEMORATION OF THE COMPLETION OF THE 60TH YEAR OF THE REIGN OF HER MAJESTY QUEEN VICTORIA. JUNE 22ND 1897.

The Jubilee clock plaque on St Mary Magdalen church. (Author)

The western side of the High Street looking north. (Basildon Heritage)

The southern end of High Street looking north, *c*.1912. The police station now stands where the trees are. (Basildon Heritage)

Lion Lane, c.1910. Some development has taken place, although the area still feels rural. (Basildon Heritage).

Kelly's Post Office Directory for Billericay in 1894 states that 'a small market is held on Tuesdays, chiefly for pigs'. This did not survive to the end of the century; the last recorded date is 1899. Associated fairs had ceased in 1887, towards the end of their existence being removed from the High Street to the Sun Corner, now occupied by the police station.

During the Second South African or Boer War the Relief of Ladysmith in March 1900 was followed in May by the Relief of Mafeking. Billericay celebrated both of these events with gusto. According to the *Essex Weekly News*, flags were displayed on the roof of the Town Hall and on private houses in the High Street when news of the Relief of Ladysmith reached the town, and much joy was expressed by the inhabitants. The *Essex Chronicle* recorded the celebrations that marked the Relief of Mafeking: fog signals were let off on the railway and guns were fired, the town crier announced the news in the streets and flags were exhibited from almost every building. In the evening a procession arranged by Ernest Harrington paraded through the streets, with a band and torches, and there were bonfires. More than £5 was collected for the Reservists Fund, and the manager of Great Burstead Board School gave the children a holiday the following Monday.

Community life was strong at this time. Sporting events continued to gain significance, and the annual meeting of the Billericay Athletics Association was recognised as a general holiday throughout the district. In 1911 a Scout group was formed.

In the late 1900s the Brentwood and District Provident Co-operative Society opened a branch in the town. This originally occupied the old meeting room of the former Bull Inn, which closed in 1906, but in 1911 a permanent building was constructed across the road. For a time, from the 1880s to 1914, there was a Billericay and District Building Society.

Billericay was mentioned in a novel written in 1906, *The Invasion of 1910* by William Le Queux, in which Germany invades England. Many Essex locations are mentioned. This was one of a number of novels that were written before the First World War about an invasion of England, often but not necessarily by Germany. *The War of the Worlds* by H.G. Wells (1898), which mentions Chelmsford and Maldon among other places, is about a Martian invasion of southern England, while William Le Queux's *The Great War in England in 1897* (1894) is about an invasion of England by France and Russia, who are defeated with the help of Germany.

The weir pond, *c.*1910. (Basildon Heritage)

Gooseberry Green, *c.*1910. Note the state of the road. (Basildon Heritage)

In 1906 the Evangelical Free Church opened in Back Lane. This was associated with a Dr W. Shackleton, who later owned it and preached there for many years; Dr Shackleton returned to England from China in 1909, and remained here because of his health. After a few years in Cambridge, in 1912 he came to Billericay, continuing in general practice until 1940. Dr Shackleton was something of a character, his strong religious fervour often leading him into stormy encounters with the clergy and ministers of other denominations.

For the coronation of King George V in 1911 there was a church service and then a procession from the railway bridge to the cricket meadow, where there were sports and teas for the children. Later there was a bonfire with fireworks in the meadow near the station – and, of course, the town was decorated.

The Times of 8 January 1908 reported on the difficulties that Billericay RDC was encountering with regard to the housing of the working classes. Young people who were employed on farms and wanted to get married were deciding that it was useless waiting for houses, and consequently were migrating to towns. Villages were becoming depopulated, and when houses became dilapidated landlords were pulling them down rather than putting them into a habitable condition. New houses were rarely built. The report continued by saying that the RDC had decided to advertise for plans and estimates for four and six-bedroomed houses, and were offering a premium of 10gns to encourage competition. It concluded with the statement that other districts in Essex were in the same situation, and were watching the experiment with interest. By 1911 there was progress. It was reported in *The Times* of 30 August that the Local Government Board was prepared to sanction the erection of wooden houses by the RDC, provided that such buildings were built in accordance with local by-laws, to provide homes to be let to rural labourers and to combat overcrowding. A Mr J. Markham, a member of the RDC, was quoted as saying that the problem arose because many London pensioners and tradesmen were coming to the district and ousting labourers from their homes by offering higher rents. In his opinion the best course for the RDC was to buy existing houses whenever the opportunity arose, and reserve them for the working classes. Despite this positive news, on 13 October *The Times* reported that the RDC had changed its mind: workmen's cottages were not to be built, despite all sides admitting the need for them. Following the passing of a resolution to build cottages in six parishes, there had been protest meetings in a dozen parishes, which did not want the cottages and objected to contributing to them elsewhere. When a motion to rescind the resolution was brought,

High Street from Cottis's Bakery to St Mary Magdalen church. (Basildon Heritage)

The northern end of the High Street, 1900s. The large house at the far end is Norsey View. (Basildon Heritage)

High Street, *c.*1906. Note the chickens in the road. (Basildon Heritage)

Line up of traction engines at Barleylands Country Show. (Author)

several council members stated that they would have to vote for it because of the strength of feeling in their respective parishes. Even though the council had permission to build the cottages, the chairman admitted that because of the protests their plans would come to nothing.

It wasn't just stories of district policy that reached *The Times*. On 3 November 1913 the newspaper reported that a Billericay man, John Keeling, farmer of Crays Hall, had been fined £5 for selling beer without a licence. He had supplied beer to men with a threshing machine who were working for him, deducting the money from their wages. His defence was that the men were often a long way from a public house, so beer was carried with the traction engine that was used to power the threshing machine.

By the beginning of the twentieth century the railway was well established, and *Bradshaw's Railway Guide* for April 1910 records Billericay as being served by at least a dozen trains in both directions. However, by the beginning of 1911 there was concern being raised by the GER shareholders and in local newspapers about the poor service provided by the GER on its line from Southend to London. The GER got to work, and from 1 May the service on the line was increased, with restaurant cars being introduced on some trains. Billericay now had at least fifteen trains a day.

Chapel Street, 1900s. (Basildon Heritage)

No. 106 High Street (Oak House) in its original form. (Basildon Heritage)

The weir pond and Weir Cottages at the rear of the Rising Sun. (Basildon Heritage)

Jackson's Lane, 1911. (Basildon Heritage)

In 1912 the LTSR was taken over by the Midland Railway, who obtained powers to electrify the line from Fenchurch Street to Southend via Upminster. Unfortunately this was not carried out, partly because of the advent of the First World War.

During 1914 the first motor bus service started to Billericay, operated by the National Steam Car Company – whose buses were powered by steam rather than petrol, the fuel being naphtha oil (which during the First World War was easier to obtain than petrol). It was an extension of a service that had started running on weekdays only from Chelmsford to Galleywood in 1912 and had been extended to Stock in 1913, running on Tuesdays, Fridays and Saturdays. It ran to Billericay on the same days of the week. During the war the service was reduced to running on Tuesdays and Fridays. After the war the National Steam Car Company began to run conventional petrol-engined buses, and changed its name to the National Omnibus and Travel Company.

While it is not known when the first aeroplane flew over Billericay it seems likely that the first landing took place on 18 September 1913. *The Times* of the following day reported that a Short biplane piloted by Captain Courtney RN, which together with three other aeroplanes was being flown from Eastchurch (Kent) to Rugby, broke a piston rod just as Billericay was reached. Happily Captain Courtney and his mechanic landed safely and without injury.

At the beginning of August 1914 the First World War began – and the world was never the same again.

Billericay Rural District Council was formed in 1894 under the Local Government Act of that year. It comprised the parishes of Basildon, Brentwood, Bowes Gifford, Childerditch, Downham, Dunton, East Horndon, Great Burstead, Hutton, Ingrave, Laindon, Lee Chapel, Little Burstead, Little Warley, Mountessing, Nevendon, North Benfleet, Pitsea, Ramsden Bellhouse, Ramsden Crays, Shenfield, South Weald, Vange, West Horndon and Wickford.

As mentioned in the main body of the text, for civil purposes Billericay remained part of Great Burstead parish, while in 1899 Brentwood separated from the RDC and became a UDC in its own right.

From the evidence available it would seem that the Council held its meeting in the offices of the Board of the Poor Law Union until 1927, when the meetings appear to have moved to the Rose Hall (the former Congregational church Sunday school building) in Chapel Street.

In 1934 the RDC became Billericay UDC. The parishes of Hutton, Ingrave and South Weald were transferred to Brentwood UDC, while Mountnessing and parts of the parishes of Downham, Ramsden Bellhouse, Ramsden Crays and Shenfield were transferred to Chelmsford RDC. At the same time part of the parish of Buttsbury in Chelmsford RDC and parts of Corringham, Fobbing and Langdon Hills in Orsett RDC were transferred to the new UDC.

eleven

THE FIRST WORLD WAR

At first, most people thought that the war was going to be short. At the meeting of the Board of Guardians on 11 August the following resolution was carried: 'That the Guardians deeply deplore the unhappy state of war into which this country has been plunged and hope and pray that a successful conclusion may be speedily attained.' At first life went on much as normal, but the war began to make itself felt – sometimes in unexpected ways. For example, at a meeting of Billericay RDC on 11 August it was stated that Dr Wells, the medical officer, had gone away with the Territorials and that Dr Dunlop was acting as his deputy. On 12 August the Billericay Harriers and Athletic Association unanimously decided to abandon its athletics meeting on 20 August on account of the war. There were local recruitment drives almost instantly, and troops were stationed in the area – the 6th Warwickshire Regiment and the 5th Battalion Royal Norfolk Regiment. According to photographs, troops were encamped on fields near the Isolation Hospital. On one occasion at least, in 1915, Mountnessing public goods siding between Shenfield and Billericay was used for the entrainment of troops. The workhouse was used as a billet for them, while later in the war German prisoners were also housed in part of the building. A YMCA centre was established in the town. There was the fear of the Germans invading and information was issued to all householders of what to do if the Germans invaded. The last surviving windmill was used as an observation post. In Norsey Wood the London Defence Volunteers dug a series of defensive trenches running north to south in the eastern part of the wood along the line of medieval Deerbank. This was part of the inner defence line for London.

The most important event in Billericay during the First World War was the destruction of the German airship L32 in the early hours of Sunday 24 September 1916. Bombing raids by German airships started on 19 January 1915 when two airships raided Great Yarmouth, killing two people and injuring sixteen.

The first raid against London took place on 31 May, killing seven and injuring thirty-five. Casualties in the early days were heavy, as people used to stay out to watch the airships rather than take shelter. Counter-measures against the raiders included the imposition of blackouts at night, anti-aircraft guns and searchlights, and home defence airfields, such as North Weald Bassett, Rochford and Hornchurch. There were also emergency landing grounds: aeroplanes were in their infancy and not very reliable; engine failure was a common occurrence, and running short of fuel was another hazard. Although each emergency landing ground was allocated to one of the Home Defence Squadrons, they could be used by any squadron for an emergency landing. The nearest to Billericay was at Hall Lane, Mountnessing; it was established in April 1916, when the airship raids were causing a real panic. The landing ground, at 21 acres the smallest in Essex, sloped steeply to the north with a wood on one side and undulating fields falling away in all directions on the other three sides. It was not an ideal location – but there was a panic on. The landing ground was opened, according to Paul A. Dowsett's *Fields of the First* (1997), for the use of No. 39 Home Defence Squadron, who were stationed at North Weald Bassett as part of the 49th Wing South East Area. It has not been established what facilities were provided at the site, but there were no ground signals for landing aircraft. There must have been a telephone (although the number is not known), as this would have allowed the troops manning the site to receive orders to place landing flares. When it was realised that Mountnessing was not a good location, another was established at Palmers Farm, near Shenfield. This opened in September 1916, and Mountnessing closed three months later – there having been, as far as can be established, no landings at the site.

On the night of 23 September 1916 twelve airships in two groups set out from their base in Nordholz, Germany. Eight made for the Midlands and Northern England and the others (L31, 32, 33 and 34) for London and the Home Counties. L32, commanded by Oberleutnant Werner Peterson, made landfall over England at Dungeness and headed towards London. A heavy barrage from anti-aircraft guns forced Peterson to abandon his plan, and he dropped his bombs between Aveley and South Ockendon – or, some sources say, in the Thames. Second Lieutenant Frederick Sowrey of the Royal Fusiliers attached to the Royal Flying Corps was on patrol in a BE2c aircraft from Sutton's Farm, Hornchurch, and was attracted by searchlights to the east that were revealing the cigar shape of an airship scudding through patches of clouds. When the searchlights lost their quarry the airship slipped away. At 12.45am he again saw an airship, heading east, so climbed to 13,000ft and gave chase. He quickly overhauled L32 and opened fire. His first and second sweeps failed to produce results, so he reloaded with incendiary ammunition. One short concentrated burst exploded into a crimson flash, and within seconds the airship was a blazing inferno. Elated by his achievement, Sowrey returned to Sutton's Farm. Later he was awarded the DSO for his action.

This is, however, not quite the whole story. Robert Miller Christy was living in Chignal St James at the time, and wrote in the *Essex Review* for April 1926:

> About twenty minutes to one, I was awakened – not by the explosions [of distant bombs] (which had ceased temporarily), but by the excited crowing of the pheasants in the woods round the house and the loud bellowing of the cows in the neighbouring farm. I knew 'something was up' (in more than the colloquial sense), so I arose and went to the window. At once I heard a Zeppelin – L32, as was ascertained later – passing in front of the house, a mile or so distant, coming from the direction of London and proceeding east or south-east. I could not see it in the darkness; but came to the conclusion that it would not be passed as 'fit' by a medical tribunal; for it lacked the familiar note of a healthy Zeppelin and was both 'wheezy' and slow of gait. I decided that it had been 'pricked' (as one would say of small winged game) in the London district, where the guns had been so busy. It passed slowly into the distance and I went back to bed.

This suggests that the anti-aircraft guns had done some damage to the L32 – and this fact was later confirmed.

The people of east London and south-east Essex were denied sleep that night because of police whistles sounding the air-raid alert, followed by gunfire. Some took shelter in air-raid shelters, but others stayed up to watch the progress of the searchlights and to watch the duel. Over the noise of the airship's engines they heard the noise of the machine gun of the aircraft, and saw red tracer bullets smash into L32. As the fire took hold a mighty cheer arose. At North Ockendon Mary Blakeley saw it pass directly over her house – so close that she was aware of the 'heat and the stench'. At Kynochtown munitions works near Corringham, Catherine Brown and her colleagues saw the blazing hulk of the airship slowly sink to the ground. At Hutton, Helen Dixon heard the screams of the crew as they were incinerated. Young Lewis Donald Jarvis of Stock wrote in his diary: 'I watched the Zeppelin being hit by a shot from one of our aeroplanes, and drifting in flames low over the village towards Billericay.

The whole village was lit up (and the amount of traffic through the village all the day following was enormous).' It was said that when L32 was burning a newspaper could be read up to 20 miles away, and that the sky was lit up for 60 miles around. The Rev. Andrew Clark in Great Leighs wrote in his diary (published as *Echoes of the Great War*) that the light was so bright you could have seen to pick up a needle from the road.

The airship fell to the ground in a field of turnips. To Miller Christy, it appeared that L32 fell very deliberately and by stages; at certain points it almost seemed to be stationary, blazing furiously – black smoke above the flames. Then blazing petrol seemed to fall out, after which the airship blazed more furiously. This was repeated several times before it settled down behind the crest of a distant hill, at Snail's Farm, Great Burstead. Miller Christy thought the fall lasted just two minutes. The crew of twenty-two were all dead; only Oberleutnant Werner Peterson had reached the ground alive, but he died immediately after being found. The wreck was 250yds long and 25yds in diameter. In the end, it took a fortnight to clear away the wreckage, and longer than that to repair the damaged hedges and gates.

People who lived nearby were first to arrive; next came the police and the fire brigade. One of the first police officers on the scene was Inspector Allen Ellis of Billericay, who watched the airship crash and cycled to the site, arriving ten minutes later. Another early arrival was Sergeant Wolverton, also of Billericay. They were soon joined by special constables from Billericay, Little Burstead and Great Burstead and constables from Hutton and Brentwood, as well as one from Chelmsford. The special constables under Chief Special Constable E.M. Magor were given the task of guarding the bodies of the crew, remaining on duty until daybreak. By that time Captain Ffinch, commander of the Essex Special Constabulary, had arrived, together with some Irish Guards who were stationed in the vicinity. The special constables handed over the duty of guarding the crash site to them.

Then all hell broke loose. News of the crash spread by word of mouth and telegraph, and by four o'clock, still some hours before daylight, a large crowd had gathered, some from London. Some were still in their nightclothes, having followed the glow of the fire for a greater distance than they expected. There were Londoners still attired for the theatre, the men in top hats and tails and the women in evening dress. By mid-morning (according to Miller Christy) thousands of troops had formed a closed circle round the airship, and no one was allowed to approach within a couple of hundred yards or so – but

Above An aerial view of crashed Zeppelin L32, September 1916. (Basildon Heritage)

Right Troops inspecting the imprint of the body of the captain of the crashed Zeppelin. (Basildon Heritage)

many people had already been very close to the wreckage. Mrs Izzard, the wife of W.P.D. Izzard, the garden expert of the *Daily Mail*, who lived in Billericay, was one. Driven back by the heat, she lost a shoe – and when this was discovered it led to the rumour that there had been a woman on board. Overhead a British airship patrolled backwards and forwards. To Miller Christy it 'seemed as if half the population of Essex and East London were already there, and newcomers were arriving continuously. Motors were parked in side roads and cycles were almost stacked in cottage gardens to the great profit of the occupants.' According to *The Times* of 25 September, tradespeople (probably from London) who had motor delivery vans took large family parties to see the crash. Some Australian soldiers who were stationed nearby hired a taxicab to go and see it. Quick precautions were put in train to prevent souvenir hunters making away with anything detachable, but this wasn't completely successful. Here is what Cliff Cottee of Stock wrote many years after the event:

Early in War 1 Zeppelin brought down Billericay Saturday night. Set on fire. Everyone in it died. Next Sunday morning in chapel not very interested in the service. Soldiers marching past – attracted us youngsters. Home to dinner. Then off to see the Zep. We went nearly to South Green. Fragments of the Zep were strewn for quite long distances. Aluminium chips, burnt silk cord, and cloth. Quite a time it took, before getting home to a late tea. One incident. Mr J. Madle from Stock brought his sister Emma to see the Zep in his horse and cart. When Jimmy got to a corner of the road a lorry came along with the rudder of the Zep. This piece was longer than the motor carrying it, and on the corner as the motor turned the rudder swung round over the top of Madles cart. Emma ducked in time to save her head being knocked off. A memorable day. Stock boys sold pieces of the Zep and made quite a bit of cash.

They were not the only ones. Occasionally fragments of the airship's aluminium framing were found, and a considerable trade was done with the latecomers. One vendor, a Londoner who had gathered a bag full, was charged shortly afterwards at a neighbouring police court for being in possession of these fragments and 'neglecting to forthwith communicate the fact to a military post or to a police constable contrary to the Defence of the Realm Regulations'. A Billericay man who had taken pieces of the Zeppelin as souvenirs had them confiscated, and was prosecuted. A young lad named Freeman got away with a chart from the airship. He gave it to his employer, who sent it to London to be framed before the police came to confiscate it. Corporal Albert Harrington on guard duty was ordered to stop passing cars and search them. In one he found a bag full of Zeppelin parts and one of its wheels, which he immediately confiscated. Even soldiers sold souvenirs. The Rev. Andrew Clark records that one of the soldiers stationed in Great Leighs drove the wife of his lieutenant to the crash site and, being in uniform, strolled up to the cordon of soldiers stationed to keep the public away. When the sentries changed he picked up some fragments, and put them in his pockets as well as under the collar of his tunic. When he got back to camp the next day he made about £1 from selling them. A man from Billericay Camp who found the Zeppelin's compass refused an offer of £5 for it from a Londoner.

Another form of enterprise, this time almost legitimate, was carried out by a man who went to the Union Hunt Kennels at Great Burstead and acquired a lump of horsemeat. After taking it home and cooking it, he sold 'beef' sandwiches to visitors for 2s 6d each. He wasn't the only one to provide refreshments. Vendors of lemonade and other soft drinks set up temporary booths at the wayside, and made large profits.

Soon the Great Eastern Railway put on six special trains for sightseers. The station staff at Billericay were kept exceedingly busy, and the station even ran out of tickets.

Some people took a rather different view of the whole thing. The reporter of the *New York Times* went to a farmhouse near where the L32 fell to find the grandfather of the family eating a hearty breakfast. The old man said, 'I do think as there do be too much fuss over these 'ere Zepps.'

The bodies were put in a shed that served as a temporary mortuary. Looting still took place: the commander's silk waistcoat and all his buttons were cut off, while from other bodies that had not been badly burned a fur collar and fur gloves, and possibly a gold watch, were taken. The airmen were buried in Great Burstead churchyard on 27 September. The commander was given his own grave, but the rest were interred communally. There they remained until the 1960s, when they were exhumed and taken to the German Military Cemetery in Cannock, Staffordshire.

There were some people who felt sorry for the L32's crew. Catherine Brown said years later that some of her work colleagues who had visited the crash site reported that some of the crewmen looked only about fourteen. 'We could not help but feel for their mothers in Germany.'

After the end of the war, a report in *The Times* of 17 December 1919 stated that it was proposed to build a memorial and thanksgiving church in Billericay, where the Zeppelin had been brought down, as the current church was inadequate and there was no vicarage. Although a fund had been started, nothing came of this proposal.

The airship L32 was not the only German flying machine brought down in the area during the war. On the night of 28–9 January 1918 a Gotha aeroplane was shot down at Frund's Farm, between Stock and Wickford, by two pilots from No. 44 Home Defence Squadron, based at Hainault Farm and flying Sopwith Camels. The three crew members of the Gotha were killed.

Billericay was deeply affected by the First World War in many other ways, as all communities were. In the middle of 1915, following a decline in the number of men volunteering to join the forces, the government ordered a national register of men and women in order to ascertain the number of those who were available for war service. The organisation of this register

Troops inspecting the remains of the crashed Zeppelin. (Basildon Heritage)

Another view of the crashed Zeppelin. (Basildon Heritage)

was put into the hands of local councils. Pressure grew for the introduction of conscription, although some regarded this as against the liberal principles on which British society was supposedly based. As an alternative, in October 1915 the so-called Derby Scheme was launched – in which men aged between eighteen and forty-one were invited to register their willingness to serve in the armed forces when needed. This had little effect in increasing the number of men joining the forces, and in March 1916 conscription was introduced for single men aged between eighteen and forty-one who were not widowers with dependent children, ministers of religion, medically unfit, engaged in essential work or with a conscientious objection to military service. In the following years this scheme was extended, despite some opposition.

Those who had a conscientious objection to joining the armed forces were able to state their case before a local military tribunal. There were twenty-six and a half of these in Essex, the half being shared with Suffolk – and one of them was in Billericay. A decision from the Billericay tribunal made it into *The Times*, which on 18 December 1916 reported that the exemption from military service of hunt servants had been withdrawn.

Rationing was introduced from late 1917, with sugar being the first foodstuff to be affected. Sugar retailers were registered, and householders had to register with one of them. Rationing cards were issued to all householders, and in Billericay there were 3,000 applications for these. When milk was rationed infants and invalids received priority vouchers. In February 1918 the rationing of other foods was introduced throughout London and the Home Counties, and was extended to the rest of the country in July. The weekly allowances were 1½lb of meat per person, 4oz of butter or margarine, 8oz of sugar and 7lb of bread for a man and 4lb of bread for a woman. By the beginning of October 1917 the food control committees were pegging milk prices, but this was met with opposition from the retailers. At Brentwood and Billericay milk retailers threatened that they would only make one delivery of milk a day if their request for an increase in the price of milk was rejected. The dispute dragged on through 1918, beyond the Armistice and into 1919. Rationing finally ceased in November 1920 – with sugar being the last foodstuff to return to normal supply.

The railways in the latter stages of the war services were severely pruned, with large gaps outside rush hours. Fares were increased to reduce the demand for travel. *The Times* of 10 January 1917 reported that the Billericay Board of Guardians had protested against the large increase in train fares.

Even the weather was unkind during the war. There was severe snow in early 1915, 1916, 1917 and 1918. After a bad snowfall in January 1918 Stock Brook flooded, and the main road from Billericay to Stock was impassable.

Not all was doom and gloom, however. In February 1917 the National Steam Car Company advertised special trips on Sunday afternoons (weather permitting) from Chelmsford bus terminus to Stock for 6d and Billericay for 1s; children's fares were half this amount. The following year even these excursions were suspended for the duration of the war.

During the war the matter of working-class homes came up again. At the end of April and the beginning of May 1918 Billericay Rural District Council adopted a proposal to build about 150 homes, in line with government suggestions.

On Monday 11 November 1918 the war came to an end. There was much rejoicing, and much sadness over those who had been lost. According to the *Essex County Chronicle* of Friday 15 November 1918, the end of the war was announced at eleven o'clock by the sounding of the siren on the police station, and flags were displayed throughout the town. In the evening the Scouts paraded through the town with their band, and the following evening a bonfire was lit. At its meeting on the 12th the Rural District Council made the following declaration: 'That the Council resolve to record its deep thankfulness to Almighty God that the Great European War has victoriously terminated and that peace is now imminent.' At their meeting on the 12th the Board

The war memorial.
(Basildon Heritage)

of Guardians expressed 'a feeling of gratitude at the consummation of our efforts and the efforts of our Allies in bringing the awful war to a successful termination. The fate of the Kaiser and his followers would be a lesson to all who desire to follow in their footsteps. Now there was a great work before us All – Parliamentary, municipal and actual – it is hoped that the spirits shown would be similar to that of our brave men who brought the war to such a successful end – namely the spirit of self-sacrifice.'

Like everywhere else, Billericay wanted to construct a war memorial, and a committee was formed to this end. The memorial, which is situated in the High Street in front of St Mary Magdelen at the junction with Chapel Street, was unveiled on Sunday 16 October 1921 by Major-General Sir William Thwaites, KCMG, CB, with a guard of honour of forty ex-servicemen under RSM J.W. Wheatley. It was dedicated by the rural dean, the Rev. S.L. Brown, also the Rector of Fryerning, and lists the names of the sixty-two men from Billericay who lost their lives. It was handed over to Great Burstead Parish Council by Mr W.J. Curtis on behalf of the memorial committee, and the Vicar of Billericay, the Rev. W.S. Smith, offered prayers of thanksgiving.

THE DEATH OF COMMANDER PETERSEN
AND THE L32'S BALLAST BOOK

A document from the wreckage of the L32 and a description of the last moments of the airship's commander did not come to light until over fifteen years after the airship's destruction – on its thirteenth voyage. In January 1932 the *Daily Mail* recounted how the ballast book of the Zeppelin had come to light. It had been found by a local man who was one of the first, if not the first, to reach the blazing wreckage. He saw a man staggering out of the wreckage, his clothes on fire and carrying a large book. Suddenly he pitched on his face, shouting 'Dreizehn' (thirteen) three times. He was Commander Petersen, the only member of the crew to escape immediate death. As he jumped clear he must have remembered the superstition attaching to thirteen. Another source records that he had a broken neck.

The existence of the book was revealed to a city businessman, to whom it was shown by Captain J. Crossley, a retired officer of the 9th Lancers. Captain Crossley had obtained it from a friend, who had obtained it in turn from the widow of the original finder.

Each page of the ballast book contained a detailed plan of the airship, with the distribution of weight for each bay. For every flight the amount of fuel, oil, water-ballast, gas and bombs had been filled in with a pencil, each entry dated and signed by the commander – except for the thirteenth page, which was not complete. The commander didn't live to sign it at the end of the voyage.

Experts declared that had the book been taken to the authorities as soon as it was found it would have been of immense value, because of the secrets it contained.

twelve

THE LONG TRUCE

Unfortunately the end of hostilities did not bring an end to all suffering. The war was swiftly followed by the Spanish Influenza epidemic, and its attendant loss of life: up to 250,000 people died in Britain.

Life soon began to return to normal after the dark days of the war. Sport, for example, began to regain its earlier prominence. After a suspension during wartime, Billericay Town FC entered the Mid-Essex League, and remained a fixture until 1947. Similarly after suspension during the First World War, Billericay Cricket Club recommenced playing in 1919.

The town continued to expand. At Queen's Park sales of building plots continued into the 1920s. The purchasers were mainly Londoners, who visited on day trips and decided to build weekend cottages or invest in land. Plots were sold for as little as £5 each. Only a small percentage were built on, and the whole area became a network of muddy, unlit, deeply rutted unadopted roads, impassable to motor vehicles, with a few houses and bungalows scattered in a vast area of overgrown scrubland.

The scheme for local authority houses to be built by Billericay RDC had run into difficulties by the middle of May 1920, when local housing schemes were being delayed through a lack of tenders. Advertisements for these had been widely published, but not a single application was received. By August, however, the RDC was considering tenders for houses in Pitsea and four other parishes; the lowest received was over £1,200 per house. The chairman referred to the great need for houses – but said that the tenders were impossibly high.

Another indication of a growing population was the formation of the Roman Catholic Diocese of Brentwood in 1917; this covered the whole of Essex. The reason for Brentwood rather than Chelmsford was that the first bishop, Bishop Ward, was a railway enthusiast. He had wanted Ilford while Rome had wanted Chelmsford; Brentwood was the compromise. In 1918 a Scotsman, Father

High Street with a wonderful array of motor vehicles, c.1930. (Basildon Heritage)

Aloysius Roche, arrived to take charge of the parish of the Holy Redeemer in Billericay. He remained parish priest for forty-five years, until 1966 (the longest-serving parish priest in the town so far). During his time he was elevated to the rank of monsignor and became something of a celebrity, in demand as a guest speaker in many London churches and appearing on the BBC. In 1963 he published a history of the Catholic Church in Billericay. He died in 1968. It was only in 1920 that it was decided to finish the church, as the number of Catholics in the town was increasing. Work was completed in 1926, the total cost being £1,500.

Transport soon returned to normal after the war, with Pullman cars being introduced on some of the Southend rail services in 1920; these lasted until 1924. In 1923, under the government enforced grouping of the railways, the Great Eastern Railway became part of the London and North Eastern Railway (LNER). Also in 1920, in mid-May, the National Omnibus and Travel Company's buses began to run from Chelmsford to Billericay daily – albeit only two a day at first, except for three on Sundays. In the same year the National and Westcliff-on-Sea Motor Charabanc Company Ltd applied for a licence to run buses from Chelmsford to Southend via Billericay, Wickford and Rayleigh. The service started on 3 June 1921. By 1923 the service from Chelmsford that terminated at Billericay had been extended to Laindon. Competition was increasing. From the early 1920s a company called Campbell's introduced a service between Billericay and Laindon, while in 1921 Mr J.F. Hinton started Laindon and District Motor Services – whose

Holy Redeemer church, between the wars. (Basildon Heritage)

Holy Redeemer church, c.2008. (Author)

main route was a circular one from Laindon station to the Pipps Hill area, supplemented by buses to Chelmsford, Wickford or Romford on market days and to Brentwood on Saturdays. One of these at least, the Chelmsford route, passed through Billericay. In the same year Tom Webster of Laindon started cartage work in the Laindon area using a Model T Ford lorry, which he converted to a charabanc at weekends. He later ran in competition with Laindon and District Motor Services, operating under the name of Old Tom Motor Service, and either took over or succeeded them. His routes included one from Laindon to Brentwood via Great Burstead and Billericay.

In 1919 the Congregational church, realising that the following year was the tercentenary of the sailing of the *Mayflower*, decided to commemorate the event. The church's pastor, the Rev. R.G. Coveney obtained the support of the South Essex branch of the Congregational Union and also the Free Church Council, which was arranging *Mayflower* celebrations on a national scale. Subsequently a *Mayflower* Celebrations Committee appointed by the Essex Congregational Union decided that Billericay should be one of the celebration centres throughout the tercentenary year. The main event was the erection of a wall tablet in the church and the renovation of the interior. According to

The Times of 17 July 1920, the tablet was to be unveiled by the American ambassador to Britain, but this did not happen; it was unveiled in the presence of many American visitors by Mrs Sandford Bissell, a descendant of William Bradford, who was governor of the Plymouth colony for much of the time between 1621 and 1656. Unfortunately the tablet only commemorated four of the five people from Billericay who sailed with the *Mayflower*; the fifth name was not added until the 350th anniversary in 1970.

Also in 1919 a decision was made to build a *Mayflower* memorial hall in the town to commemorate those who had sailed from Billericay. A fund was established, but it was 18 November 1926 before the foundation stone was laid, by which time the Rev. R.G. Coveney had been succeeded by the Rev. Henry Welch (in 1925). The stone was laid by A. Owen Ward, JP, Trust Secretary of the Essex Congregational Union. The hall was completed in just over six months, and the formal opening and dedication service took place on 21 May 1927, conducted by the Rev. H. Ross Williamson, Moderator of the Eastern Province of the Congregational Union. Mr J.C. Meggitt, Chairman of the Congregational Union of England and Wales, formally declared the building open. A sermon was preached by the Rev. D.W. Langridge, Chairman of the Essex Congregational Union, the memorial tablet was unveiled by Mr Campbell Lee, chairman of the American Society in London, and a prayer was offered by the Rev. Henry Welch, Pastor of Billericay Congregational church. The building had three rooms named after missionary pioneers – Dr David Livingstone, Dr William Carey and Dr Robert Morrison. The total cost was said to be £4,000, of which more than half had been raised.

After the war there was an attempt to restart the town market. A newspaper report of 2 July 1920 stated that the livestock market was to be re-established on a new site, known as the Chantry Barn. There were said to be stalls, stables, barns and other outbuildings and a paddock, as well as a site suitable for a sale yard. The new market didn't last long, as in December 1922 it was announced that J.E. Ladbrook was to hold a sale of furniture at the market at the back of the Chequers daily until further notice. A more successful market was run for many years between the wars at the corner of Norsey Road and Crown Road, but it closed at the outbreak of the Second World War.

The town hospital was also developed in these years. In 1924 shelters were added for tubercular patients. The bell and the clocktower were demolished in the 1930s. The county architect's report at this time stated that 'The roofs generally in the older part are in doubtful condition and expenditure will have to be incurred to recondition them'. A new single-storey infirmary was built in 1925, and the Board of Guardians arranged for a loan of £2,000 to add a first floor in 1927. A nurses' home was built in 1925, and an operating theatre was added when the new infirmary was completed. Also in 1927 an administrative block was built.

In 1917 the Billericay branch of the Women's Institute had been founded, and in 1924 the Institute opened a hall in St Edith's Lane. Originally it had a seating capacity of 300, but with alterations over the years this has increased. Currently it

A bus timetable commencing 15 May 1920, which is believed to be the start date of daily bus services to Billericay. (Alan Osborne collection).

is available for meetings and concerts of all descriptions, and has been used for exhibitions, while until the opening of the public library in 1950 part of it was used as a public library for an hour on two days a week.

In 1926 the Billericay Residents' Association was formed. It remained active until the outbreak of the Second World War, and then became dormant until just before the war ended. Perhaps community feeling was a little lacking in some quarters: when the Congregationalist minister, the Rev. R.G. Coveney, was conducting his last service in the town on 29 March 1925, Dr Shackleton of the Evangelical Free Church, who was something of a character, commented that Mr Coveney's ministry had been like the blind leading the blind.

Controversy continued in 1926, when on 5 June it was reported in the *Manchester Guardian* that the Chantry House (Christopher Martin's supposed old home) had been sold the previous day in London for the sum of £10,000, to an American with large oil interests. The house was to be removed to Boston and re-erected there. The *Daily Chronicle* of 5 June reported that the owner of the house since 1919, Mr C.H. King, had said that the sale was not definitely settled, after a week of negotiations. News of the possible sale spread, and began to arouse comment. On 7 June a letter from Mr C.F. Jerdein of Warwick

Square, London SW1 was published in *The Times*, asking why the Society for the Preservation of Historic Buildings had not protested. On 9 June there was another letter on the subject, this time from Samuel Looker of Billericay, who wrote that steps should be taken to prevent the sale of the house and its re-erection in America. He described the plans as 'vandalism'. Also on 9 June, this time in Parliament, Sir Henry Slesser, MP for Leeds South East, asked Captain Hacking, parliamentary under secretary in the Home Office, if he was aware that four ancient buildings had been exported to America that year, and that Billericay's Chantry House was under threat. He asked if the Office of Works lacked the power to interfere with the destruction of ancient buildings, and whether steps would be taken to prevent similar exports in future. Captain Hacking replied that the problem wasn't legislation but finance. Legislation would be no good if Parliament was not prepared to allocate a sufficient sum of money to purchase historic houses. Putting a contrary point of view, Arthur Wilson of London wrote to *The Times* to ask if it was not 'false sentiment' to agitate for the retention of the house in Billericay, asking who had heard of it until the recent news. To the British the house was of no significance, but the Americans would treasure it with reverence.

An announcement regarding the sale of Chantry House appeared in *The Times* on 24 June, and in local papers. Besides the house, there were 'about 30 acres of freehold land adjacent to the Main Street affording many picturesque

The Mayflower Hall was built in the late 1920s to commemorate the *Mayflower* settlers from Billericay. (Author)

Western Road, c.1925. (Basildon Heritage)

sites available for the erection of Bungalows and Villa Residences and a Site suitable for a Cinema or Concert Hall'. On 9 July the newspaper reported that it had been sold by Messrs Talbot and White for £850. The new owner was Fred G. Burrell, a solicitor of Chelmsford, Essex – not Chelmsford, Massachusetts. By 1927 the Kings had left their home for a nearby bungalow.

Mr King had previously been indirectly involved in a project for a cinema. In 1925 it was reported that a cinema was to be erected in a prominent part of the High Street, on land owned by Mr King of Chantry Farm, at a cost of £8,000. The 800-seat cinema was to have a lofty tower crowned by a glowing ball of light, which would be visible for many miles around. Because the site was 400ft above sea level, the ball was going to be considerably higher than the dome of St Paul's Cathedral, and the light from it would be visible from London on one side and the sea on the other; it would be a beacon over the Thames estuary, visible from Southend and beyond. But things didn't go as planned. In 1927 the person responsible for the plan, together with a cinema operator, was sentenced to twelve months' imprisonment for conspiring to obtain £250 from a sheet metalworker by false pretences. The unfortunate gentleman had answered an

advertisement for a partner in a cinema business, and the two accused told him that they owned shares in a concern called the Billericay Cinema Ltd, which they wished to sell. The victim handed over his life savings, and then discovered that no such business had been registered.

Billericay was usually a peaceable place, as it had been through much of its history. It was all the more of a shock, therefore, when on 27 September 1927, just before 6am, the body of PC George Gutteridge was discovered by Bill Ward, a Post Office worker, near Howe Green. PC Gutteridge was beside the road, wearing his full uniform and cape, with his helmet and notebook beside him and his pencil still in his hand, having been shot four times in the face. Detective Inspector Crockford from Romford took up the investigation. It was discovered that a a blue four-seater Morris Cowley motor car belonging to Dr Edward Lovell had been stolen from his garage in London Road, Billericay. The car was eventually spotted in a narrow passage in Brixton, and when the police investigated they discovered a cartridge case in it. It looked as though PC Gutteridge's murder was linked to the stolen car as its mileometer indicated that it had been driven 42 miles – the distance from Dr Lovell's garage

Tanfield Drive, between the wars. (Basildon Heritage)

to Brixton. Eventually two suspects, Frederick Browne and Patrick Kennedy, were arrested. Eventually they were convicted and hanged. While Kennedy admitted his part in the killing, Browne went to the gallows protesting his innocence. Billericay policemen attended PC Gutteridge's funeral at Warley.

It is interesting to note that there were a number of false leads reported in the press. One of them indicates, perhaps, what Billericay was like at this time. Originally the police were looking for three men who were not locals, but had been seen in the Red Lion the night before the crime. Victor Fuller, the landlord, was quoted in the *Manchester Guardian*: 'I am not suggesting that they were suspicious characters, but they were strangers. We know strangers in this little town at once. They were not "polished"; I would not call them "saloon bar" customers. It might have been a coincidence that they were here the night that the Doctor's car disappeared.' Which it was …

Road transport continued to develop, with a complex network of small-scale bus companies, based in London and Essex, running competing routes. New Empress Saloons, which became the City Motor Omnibus Company, Service Saloons Ltd, Westcliff-on-Sea Motor Services Ltd, the Wickford Carriage Company, Patten's Coaches, the National Omnibus Company (which

High Street with the Red Lion on the left and the Town Hall on the right, 1920s. (Basildon Heritage)

The junction of High Street and Chapel Street, *c.*1930. (Basildon Heritage)

became the Eastern National Omnibus Company) and Ongar and District Motor Services all operated in or near Billericay – and mergers, takeovers and bankruptcies contributed to an ever-changing pattern of provision, and much duplication! Following the formation of the London Passenger Transport Board in 1933, all road and railway passenger services within its area, with the exception of those operated by the four main line railway companies, had to be operated by the Board, which brought yet more changes.

In about 1928 or 1929 Brentwood gained its own bus company, when Mr W.H. Malden started Brentwood and District Motor Services Ltd. Its first service ran from Brentwood to Hutton (Bracken Bank). Shortly afterwards another route was added: from Brentwood to Laindon via Billericay and Little Burstead. In April 1936 the company was acquired by the City Coach Company, remaining a separate entity until it was finally absorbed in December 1940. In May 1936 the City Coach Company acquired the previously mentioned Old Tom Motor Service.

As the town grew in stature, educational provision increased. In 1927, for example, St John's independent school was founded by Walter Victor Summers; it is situated in the Stock Road. It was opened on Saturday 21 January 1928 by Dr Joseph Douglas Wells. In *Kelly's Directory* for 1914 Dr Wells OBE is described as physician, surgeon, medical officer of health to the Billericay Rural District Council and medical officer to the Workhouse and Isolation Hospital; later he became medical officer of health to the Urban District Council. The first pupils arrived at the school on Tuesday 24 January 1928.

It wasn't just new schools that were built. In the 1920s Miss Georgina Archer of Little Burstead felt that St Mary Magdalen's church was too small, and also required a hall, so in her will she left land in Laindon Road for a new church. The parish could not afford this, but built the proposed hall instead. The Archer Memorial Hall was designed by a local architect, T.A. Pole, and opened in 1930. It was used not only for church activities but also for public meetings, ballet shows, sports events and theatrical performances. One such was Gilbert and Sullivan's *The Mikado*, which was performed at the Archer Hall in 1930 – the first production by Billericay Operatic Society, which had been founded the previous year. The society changed its name to Billericay Musical Theatre Group in September 2004.

At the same time as new landmarks appeared, old ones vanished. In 1929 the surviving windmill collapsed during a severe gale. The roundhouse at the base

The Archer Hall, built in 1930. (Basildon Heritage)

The ruins of Billericay windmill, *c*.1930. (Basildon Heritage)

of the mill remained for a while, but was subsequently demolished. The main post, quarter bars and crosstrees standing on their brick piers remained until 1971–2, when the decaying substructure collapsed.

Administratively things were changing too. In 1930 the workhouse became the Public Assistance Institution, initially controlled by Essex County Council. In the following decade the old receiving ward was converted into a family house for the master and matron of the workhouse/hospital. The County Medical Officer of Health for Essex stated in 1934 that Billericay's Public Assistance Institution could be developed into an excellent surgical unit. At this time there were a total of 151 beds, 66 of which were in the old infirmary. There were 108 men, 15 women and 23 children being treated, by a nursing staff of fifteen. The name St Andrew's Hospital was first used in the 1930s.

In 1931 Billericay's own newspaper was started – the *Billericay Times*. Its first edition was published on Saturday 21 November. The publisher and editor was Arthur Henry Collins, who had moved to Billericay from Hove via London. The newspaper lasted until 1965.

Modernisation continued. It was in 1930 or 1931 that mains electricity reached the town, the telephone having arrived a little before; it is not known exactly when. Roger Green tells us in *Billericay – A Pictorial History* (2005) that the telephone exchange was initially at 116 High Street, then at Glenavis, 101 High Street, from 1929 until 1952. When it was opened Billericay had twenty-four numbers, of which the station was 1.

In 1934 Billericay RDC became Billericay UDC to reflect the changing face of the area; by now the transformation from small market town to urban area was complete. The parishes of the RDC disappeared, and parts of the parish of Buttsbury in Chelmsford RDC were taken over. The rest of Buttsbury became part of the parish of Stock, and Buttsbury parish ceased to exist except for ecclesiastical purposes. The parts of Buttsbury that are in Billericay are still thus named. Changes continued: in 1938 Little Burstead was transferred to Thurrock UDC. From 1938, when the police station moved to its present accommodation, the council chamber of the UDC was in the Town Hall. Before this date it had met at the Rose Hall (the former Congregational church Sunday school building) in Chapel Street. It would seem that the meetings moved there from the workhouse after the Congregational church building became the Rose Hall in 1927, when it was sold by the church. From 1945 the council offices were in Barnsley House (98 High Street).

As Billericay developed, it was realised that the conditions of the unmade roads around the town were no longer acceptable. In the summer of 1937, according to a report in the *Sunday Chronicle*, Mr F.A. Rumsey, a member of the council and one of the leaders of a campaign for better roads in the area, stated that 'mud psychosis', brought on by the discomforts of primitive road conditions, was becoming an epidemic, and that hundreds of bungalows built in the middle of fields and reached only by rough tracks were virtually inaccessible. 'People of Billericay are living a life of banishment,' he said. 'They have got mud psychosis. Some of them are going mad through it. One man of eighty-two was taken off to the Brentwood Asylum only last week muttering "mud, mud, mud". Months of ploughing through it have upset people's nerves. They cannot wear any decent clothes and only heavy rubber boots are of any use for their legs.' It is interesting to note that this news report was picked up as far away as Australia, by the *Barrier Miner* of Broken Hill in New South Wales, in its edition of 5 June.

National events have always been celebrated lavishly in Billericay, and the Silver Jubilee of King George V and Queen Mary on 6 May 1935 was no exception. Most houses displayed the Union Jack and red, white and blue bunting, and the streets were festooned with decorations. There was a united

The Sunnymede estate, which was developed from the late 1920s. (Basildon Heritage)

service of the Protestant churches on the football field, tea for children in the Archer Hall followed by sports and entertainments for them also on the football field, dancing by the pupils of Miss Hermione Moss and in the evening a bonfire and firework display in Mr Castelden's meadow. The preparation work for this was done by the local Scout troop. There was another royal event just a couple of years later. The edition of the *Billericay Times* that gave details of the proposed celebrations for the Coronation of King George VI and Queen Elizabeth in 1937 was printed in blue ink. Because of the wet weather on the day a united service to be held in the football field on Sunday 9 May took place in the Archer Hall, where the old folk's supper the next Tuesday was also held. On Coronation Day, Wednesday 12 May, it rained again. There were teas for children in three sittings in the Archer Hall and in the evening a dance was held there. A planned pageant in Lake Meadows did not take place, although the hopeful performers gathered from 12.30; it finally went ahead when the weather was better – at Lake Meadows on the evening of 18 June. A planned bonfire and firework display at the same location was also cancelled. Until almost the end of the nineteenth century Lake Meadows had been owned by Major Thomas Jenner Spitty, before being acquired by the newly formed Billericay UDC in the mid-1930s and opened as a public park.

Mountessing Road, 1930s. (Basildon Heritage)

Billericay's population was growing apace; according to the 1931 census it was 27,708. The increasing number of children created pressure on schooling, and by 1932 classes of fifty-eight were not uncommon in Great Burstead School. Plans were made for a new secondary school, which would make more room for the juniors in the old school, and in 1937 this was opened. The new school, which cost £22,400, was built by David Marven, a contractor from Galleywood, under the direction of the Essex County Council architect, Mr J.L. Stuart. The first children arrived a year before the formal opening, which was performed on 4 May 1938 by Admiral Sir Vernon Haggard of Stock, who used the silver key handed to him by the headmaster Mr P.G. White to open the main entrance doors.

There were other festivities, some more colourful than others. For many years Rosaire's Circus had its winter quarters in Billericay, and in March 1937 *The Times* reported the wedding in the town on Saturday 20 March of Walter Shufflebottom, aged twenty-seven, the 'son of the original "Texas Bill"', and Cicely Rosaire, 'flying trapeze artist and elephant trainer'. Fred Rosaire, the circus's proprietor, gave his daughter away and the vicar of Billericay, the Rev. W.S. Smith, officiated. After the ceremony the newly weds rode away on an elephant draped in red, the bridegroom scattering pennies to cheering children.

The Times article concluded by saying that 'after the marriage the couple took part in the circus and left for the Continent for their honeymoon'. In March the following year two Rosaire children were christened: Cicely Leone Zametta Shufflebottom was the daughter of the couple who were married the previous year; the other child was Denise Elaine Rosaire. Two elephants gently proceeded along the High Street, each pushing a pram with its trunk, the children's parents riding on the elephants.

With the increasing population came improvements in facilities. In 1938 the post office moved from 104 High Street to a purpose-built building a little further along, at No. 136, while the same year saw the police station move to its present location, with residential quarters, two courts and other facilities. In the same year, on Easter Monday, 18 April, a cinema finally opened in the town, built by W. and C. French – meaning that townspeople no longer had to travel to Chelmsford, Brentwood or Southend. The first film shown at the Ritz was *Flying Down to Rio*, starring Fred Astaire and Ginger Rogers. It was on the site of the old weavers' cottages, a rather more modest building compared with the earlier proposal but even so with seating for about 650 people; it was described as an intimate little cinema where people could feel at home. At one

South Green, *c*.1925. The sign on the left advertises the Plough Inn on its original site. It was damaged by a bomb during the Second World War. (Basildon Heritage)

time there was a board inside that showed the last times of the City Coach Company's buses.

Some proposed innovations were less popular. In 1937 the *Manchester Guardian* reported that the Billericay authorities had refused to allow the building of a practice hall for a brass band near residential property, because neighbouring householders might object to the noise. The musicians appealed against the decision. The newspaper commented that while a brass band was seen as a recognised resource in Lancashire, in Essex it was seen as something like the offensive trades of soap-boiling and fish-frying.

Communication continued to improve, as the links between Billericay and the rest of Essex, and beyond, became busier. By the end of the 1930s the passenger train service was almost hourly off peak. In 1938 new colour light signalling replaced the old semaphore signals on the Southend line, and except for Wickford junction signal-box all others between Shenfield and Southend were abolished. Rail was also extensively used for goods traffic. One of the factories in Billericay manufactured galvanised sheet-metal rainwater gutters and pipes, for agricultural buildings, greenhouses and the like, and most days

The new post office, built in 1938. This photograph dates from the 1950s. (Basildon Heritage)

The new police station, built in 1938. This photograph dates from the 1950s. (Basildon Heritage)

they sent several tons of their products in small lots to different destinations. The stationmaster at this time was a Mr F.A. Allen, who came from Lavenham in Suffolk and had a very strong Suffolk accent. He was a tall and genial man who prefaced his comments with 'Cor, blarst, boy, well …'.

Bus services were improving too, with a whole host of services run by a number of companies connecting towns throughout south Essex. Many of these passed through or near Billericay. Even so, road conditions still weren't all they should have been, and at the Essex Assizes in 1939 the town was indicted for not keeping a highway in repair. The road in question was Green Lane. In the end the townspeople were acquitted, as the jury found that Green Lane was not a highway before 1835, when the liability at common law to repair highways was taken off the shoulders of a town's inhabitants. *The Times* headed their article 'The Burghers of Billericay', after the Burghers of Calais who confronted the conquering King Edward III in 1347.

FATHER ALOYSIUS ROCHE (1886–1968)

Father, later Canon, Aloysius Roche, was probably Billericay's most famous resident of the twentieth century. He was born in the Lochee area of Dundee, Scotland, in 1886, one of fifteen children in an Irish-Welsh Catholic family. He was ordained into the Redemptorists (a missionary society) in 1913. From the information given by Canon Roche in *The Catholic Church Billericay: An Historical Sketch* (c.1963) it appears that he spent the first few years of his priestly ministry as a curate at Walthamstow, before moving from the jurisdiction of the Redemptorists to the newly created diocese of Brentwood. In his own words, he 'was appointed to succeed Father (Martin) Brassil at Billericay "for the time being".' A generous and modest man, Father Roche would wear his cassock out before buying a new one.

Father Roche was very prolific, writing many books. His most popular was *A Bedside Book of Saints*, published in 1934. He was one of the first Catholic priests to become well known through radio broadcasts, and in the early 1950s he even appeared on television – his most impressive broadcast being the Stations of the Cross one Good Friday. He often used to broadcast the epilogue at the close of transmission.

Father Roche was also an animal lover and his house always had a number of cats; and at one time a family of hedgehogs. He was author of *These Animals of Ours* (1939).

In 1962 Father Roche was elevated to the rank of canon. According to his obituary in the *Catholic Herald*, he had turned the honour down many times previously. Canon Roche retired in 1966 and died in February 1968. The Canon Roche Social Centre is named after him.

thirteen

AT WAR

The build-up to the Second World War really began with the Munich Crisis of 1938. Before the formal outbreak of war, gas masks were distributed, air-raid shelters were dug, air-raid wardens were recruited and the Auxiliary Fire Service was created. Rehearsals for the evacuation of children from London and other large towns and cities took place, and there were blackout trials. Air-raid wardens and the Auxiliary Fire Service were both part of the Air Raid Precautions organisation. On 26 April Prime Minister Neville Chamberlain announced that conscription of all young men aged twenty and twenty-one for six months' military training was to be introduced immediately. Provision was made for conscientious objectors. On 1 September 1939 the Germans invaded Poland, and on the same day the evacuation of children, pregnant women and nursing mothers from London and other towns and cities began. Some of them came to Billericay.

On 3 September 1939 Chamberlain announced that as from eleven o'clock that day Britain was at war with Germany. There was an immediate blackout, and identity cards were issued. Conscription was extended to all men aged between eighteen and forty-one. By 1942 the upper age limit had been extended to fifty-one, as well as to women aged between twenty and thirty – for war work. Troops were stationed in Billericay for the duration of the war.

The _Billericay Times_ didn't say much about the start of the war. The first casualty, if he can be so described, was Jack Clarke of Sunnymede, a dispatch rider who on Wednesday 6 September was proceeding on patrol to South Green after an air-raid warning. He had difficulty turning his bicycle because his steel helmet was fastened on the front, and was thrown from the machine, receiving an injury to his hand that necessitated six stitches. He was detained in St Andrew's Hospital for a few hours, suffering from shock. St Andrew's became part of the Emergency Medical Services on the outbreak of war.

St Andrew's Hospital, developed during the Second World War. (Basildon Heritage)

For a time at the start of the war all cinemas were shut, with the last films to be shown at the Ritz being the Hitchcock classic *The 39 Steps* starring Robert Donat and Madeleine Carroll, as well as *Secrets of a Nurse*, starring Edmund Lowe, Helen Mack and Dick Foran. Cinemas reopened later, with the Ritz showing *Prison Nurse*, starring Henry Wilcoxon and Marian Marsh, and *The Last of the Newsboys*, starring Lew Ayres and Helen Mack. During the war the cinema usually played to a packed house, with queues forming down Chapel Street to St Mary Magdalen's church. Even during the heaviest air raids it remained open, although when a raid began the projectionist exhibited a scratched slide which advised the audience that they could leave the cinema if they wished to take shelter.

Railway services were pruned, while many bus services were withdrawn or restricted – with late evening buses and Sunday morning buses being casualties. Because of the importance of the Marconi works at Chelmsford, for a time there was a bus from Billericay to Chelmsford specifically for employees. Both Eastern National and the City Coach Company employed women as conductors and as drivers, with the City paying its women drivers the same as men – which was quite an innovation.

The winter of 1939–40 was cold, and in late January 1940 there was a severe blizzard that caused chaos throughout the country. At least one of the routes out of Billericay was impassable except on foot: on the road across Laindon Common to Little Burstead, there were snowdrifts through which a narrow passage for pedestrians was dug. There was very bad weather again at the beginning of 1941 and 1942.

Everyday life went on, despite the war. One significant event was the appointment of the first woman minister in the town. In January 1940 the Congregationalists invited the Rev. Dorothy F. Wilson to become their pastor. In June, however, she informed the deacons that she had been approached by Hindhead, Surrey, regarding their pastorate, and wanted to know if in the event of compulsory evacuation of the district she would be free to accept. The deacons agreed to her request. In August Miss Wilson said that it might be necessary for her to leave at short notice because of her parents' serious illness and in the autumn she did indeed leave. Her successor was George Walker – the first person to write a history of Billericay. *The Story of a Little Town* was published in 1947.

In May and June 1940 the German army invaded the Netherlands, Belgium and France, while Italy joined with Germany. There was the Dunkirk evacuation, when over 300,000 troops were rescued, and then the Battle of Britain. The Home Guard was formed, initially known as the Local Defence Volunteers. Plans for the evacuation of Billericay in the event of a German invasion were prepared, and leaflets were distributed. Roadblocks were set up, with each access road into the town centre being cut by a concrete and steel barrier, removable to allow friendly traffic to pass. They were guarded by infantry positions, and gun emplacements were built at various places in the town. The only one to survive is a spigot mortar emplacement in Norsey Road on the top of the railway embankment. South Essex south of Wickford became off limits to those who did not live there or had a very good reason to visit. Many people were evacuated from the area, as they were later in the war from Billericay.

Members of an Auxiliary Unit of the Home Guard constructed a hideout in Norsey Wood in 1940. The auxiliary units were in essence the British Resistance, and they would have operated if the Germans had invaded Britain in 1940. Fortunately this never happened, but in September 1940 there was a false alarm: members of the units went into hiding until it was over. Norsey Wood was also used for army manoeuvres, especially lorry recovery (where

Chapel Street, 1940s. (Basildon Heritage)

lorries were overturned so as to gain practice in righting them) and ammunition storage (part of the gravel pits were fenced off with barbed wire and about six trenches were dug; these storage areas were covered with curved sections of corrugated iron). A dugout was also constructed for ammunition storage.

Billericay did not escape German bombing. On 23 September 1940 a bomb detonated in the rear garden of Norsey Manor in Norsey Road. Two days later a landmine fell behind houses on the Great Burstead side of Southend Road, some 225yds south of Mill Road. One person was slightly injured and twenty-five houses were badly damaged. On 14 October 1944 a V1 flying bomb, or doodlebug as they were known, destroyed Bulstead's Farm in Southend Road at South Green. At a date which is not recorded, an enemy aeroplane machine-gunned a train travelling from Shenfield to Billericay and afterwards bombed Harts Corner, killing several people.

At the beginning of the war the Fire Brigade changed their headquarters to Sun Street garage, which was larger premises. An air-raid siren was mounted on the garage. In August 1941 the Auxiliary Fire Service and the local fire brigades were amalgamated into the National Fire Service, which covered the whole of Great Britain.

A number of buildings in Billericay were used for activities relating to the war effort. Barnsley House in the High Street was used as the local Home Guard headquarters. Burstead House Temperance Hotel in the High Street closed at the beginning of the war and the premises were used as the local Food Office. Burstead House was used by the army; captured German airmen were brought there to be interrogated. Soon after the outbreak of war the British

Legion purchased the Rose Hall, and it was used as a mess room for soldiers billeted in the town.

In June 1944 the Allies landed in Normandy, and in early May 1945 the war in Europe came to an end. Tuesday 8 May 1945 was VE Day, and the 8th and 9th were public holidays. On the Monday flags and banners of every allied nation were hung up in the High Street to honour the historic occasion, together with bunting and patriotic banners. Mr H. Harvey (the chairman of Billericay UDC) together with several councillors and the vicar formally announced the German surrender from the green outside the police station, and a large crowd listened to him read Winston Churchill's speech. Everyone joined in

One of the trenches in Norsey Wood that were dug during the Second World War. (Author)

prayers led by the Rev. W. Smith, and the formalities ended with the national anthem. As darkness fell Billericay went deliriously mad. Crowds marched through the High Street, everyone arm in arm, their way lit by two great searchlights provided by the military. Mr Bent Marshall and a band of army cadets built a huge bonfire in the Town Field, and as the sun went down this was set off by a number of practice incendiary bombs provided by the National Fire Service. Roar after roar erupted from the crowds, and scores of rockets and thunderflashes were set off at the police station. The pubs were packed, but there was more than enough beer to go round. After 11pm the crowds grew more intense around Sun Corner, where the National Fire Service had arranged dancing in the streets. Excitement was at its peak when it was announced over the loudspeakers that the time was one minute past midnight and that the war was over. Deafening cheers rang out for the royal family, the prime minister, the boys who had fought and those returning from prison camps. The loudest cheer of all was reserved for the men in Burma and the Far East, where the war continued. Total strangers shook hands and servicemen led patriotic singing. It was 1.30am before the music stopped, after the singing of Auld Lang Syne, and

Speed's Café was opened as a snack bar during the war and was modernised in 1949. (Basildon Heritage)

the crowds began to disperse. On Sunday 13 May a service was held in Lake Meadows and was conducted by the Rev. W. Smith, the Rev. G. Walker (from the Congregational church) and the Rev. W. Harris (Baptist minister).

On VJ Day in August a service was held outside the police station, led by Cllr Harvey, the Rev. W. Smith and the Rev. G. Walker. There was a dance in the High Street organised by Stanley Fisher, the proprietor of Audax Systems, with the co-operation of Mrs Elsie Savigear, the licensee of the Chequers. There was a firework display at the police station. The following night Mr A. Spiers of Electric House held a dance at St Andrew's Hospital. On Saturday, at the invitation of the stationmaster, a dance was held outside the station by Audax Systems.

It was 1957 before the names of those who had fallen in the Second World War were added to the town war memorial.

ST ANDREW'S HOSPITAL DURING THE SECOND WORLD WAR

Before the outbreak of war it was decided that hospitals in the London area would be grouped into ten sectors that radiated from the centre of London. St Andrew's became an Advance Base Sector Hospital in Sector 1 – Essex.

Emergency Medical Services huts, which were prefabricated buildings, were quickly built in sector hospitals throughout the country. St Andrew's was allocated seven huts – five as wards for servicemen and civilians and two as staff accommodation. Soldiers who were stationed at Warley Barracks were ordered to make sandbag walls to protect the wards against air raids. Air-raid shelters were also built. Medical and nursing staff from the London Hospital in Whitechapel were transferred to St Andrew's to care for the expected patients. Many of these staff were billeted in homes in Billericay; a large house in the High Street, St Edith's at the corner of St Edith's Lane, was used by nurses. Medical students and probationer nurses from the London Hospital continued their training while working at St Andrew's.

At the end of the war the London Hospital staff returned to Whitechapel. Uncertainty about the role of St Andrew's Hospital followed, although the need for a general hospital in Billericay was obvious.

St Edith's, built in about 1840, was an Ursuline convent from 1910 to 1913. The photograph was taken during the First World War. (Basildon Heritage)

fourteen

THE POST-WAR TOWN

The end of the war did not mean the end of conscription or rationing. While all women were released from service, conscription for men continued. Under the National Service Act 1948, which came into effect on 1 January 1949, all healthy men aged between seventeen and twenty-one were expected to serve in the Armed Forces for eighteen months, and remain on the reserve list for four years. In October 1950, in response to the British involvement in the Korean War, the National Service period was extended to two years. Exemption continued for conscientious objectors. National Service was abolished in 1960, and the last National Servicemen left the Armed Forces in May 1963. Rationing of food, which had begun in January 1940, lasted until the middle of 1954, with restrictions on the sale and purchase of meat and bacon being lifted at midnight on 4 July. Identity cards remained in use until 1952.

The winter of 1946–7 was one of the worst on record. Snow started to fall just before Christmas 1946 and lasted into March. On 8 February 1947, according to the *Billericay Times*, 10in of snow fell in the Billericay area and temperatures were well below freezing, with 14 degrees of frost recorded. On 28 January 1947 visibility was under 100yds, and a traveller on skis was reported on the outskirts of the town. A few days earlier a lorry bringing meat from Chelmsford to Billericay overturned near Billericay station, at the bottom of the High Street, and its load spilled into the snow. The driver and his passenger were not hurt, and two small vans took over the delivery. The *Billericay Times* reported that the town received doubly frozen meat. On 4 March a freak blizzard caused foot-high snowdrifts on the outskirts. The City Coach Company could not take to the road until 8am, instead of 4.30am, and the journey from Billericay to Wickford took forty minutes instead of twenty. There were no through London to Southend services; passengers had to change buses at Brentwood and Wickford. Billericay UDC instructed its surveyor to tell Essex County Council

The Mayflower School. (Basildon Heritage)

that it was dissatisfied with the clearing of snow in the High Roads in each of the four towns of the UDC. The UDC suggested using prisoners of war as manpower, but the reply was received that this was not possible.

To add to townspeople's misery, there was a coal shortage. Coal was the main fuel for power stations and railways, for the making of gas, for domestic heating and the manufacture of coke. In some shops candles were used instead of electricity, while some closed early. Schools and the hospital were not affected, but as the winter went on the situation got worse. One company, Messrs W.W. Balls and Sons (tool makers and plastic moulders), had to close; a couple of pubs said they were only able to open on Saturdays and Sundays. The Congregational church, which used coke for its heating, moved its services to the Mayflower Hall, which used gas. When spring finally arrived, the Billericay branch of the National Association of Local Government Officers estimated that the weather had cost the UDC £870; indirect costs were considerably more. After the terrible winter came the hot summer of 1947.

In the 1944 plan for post-war south-east England a proposal was made for a new town at Margaretting, but because it would have taken up

The International Stores, 1950s. (Basildon Heritage)

valuable agricultural land this idea fell through. As an alternative the area of uncontrolled plotland development around Langdon Hills and Pitsea, within Billericay UDC, was chosen. The proposed new town took its name from the small village of Basildon, situated between Laindon and Pitsea. Originally designated as a New Town following the New Towns Act of 1946, Basildon's status was officially confirmed in 1949. The government appointed Basildon Development Corporation, and gave it the task of transforming the designated area into a modern town. The pre-existing towns of Laindon, Pitsea and Vange, together with Lee Chapel and parts of Dunton, Langdon Hills and Nevendon, were all absorbed into the new development. The first factory in the New Town was opened in 1951, and in that same year the first tenants moved into newly completed homes. Eventually Basildon outstripped Billericay, and on 1 April 1956 Billericay UDC became Basildon UDC.

These post-war years saw administrative developments elsewhere, some more successful than others. The headquarters of the fire brigade was moved to Laindon, but after local protests and an increase in fires in Billericay it was moved back to the town. In 1948 all local fire brigades were amalgamated into the Essex County Fire Brigade.

In 1948 the National Health Service was created. Locally this meant that management of St Andrew's Hospital was taken on by the Tilbury and South East Essex Hospital Management Committee. The Isolation Hospital also became part of the NHS, being renamed St Andrew's Annex. In 1955 it was reserved exclusively for aged sick patients; later it was shut. In 1956 the inmates of the workhouse who had lived in the hospital before the 1948 National Assistance Act was implemented were transferred to residential accommodation in the community.

In 1950 Billericay became a parliamentary constituency, and in the general election of that year returned Bernard (later Sir Bernard) Braine as Conservative MP. Before this date Billericay had been part of a wider constituency: Essex South Eastern. Bernard Braine remained MP until 1955, when another Conservative, Mr R.F.S. Body, was returned.

Public services continued to increase and improve. In 1949 Essex County Council leased 97 High Street for use as a public library. This opened in 1950. In 1968 the library moved to its present location at Burghstead House, and in 1974 an extension was added – in which the library is now situated. In 1952 the telephone exchange moved from 101 High Street to new quarters behind the new post office. No. 101 was later demolished, and Woolworths (now Iceland) was built on the site.

Under the nationalisation of the railways and some bus companies in 1948, the LNER lines out of Liverpool Street became part of the Eastern Region of British Railways. The Eastern National Omnibus Company and Westcliff Motor Services were taken over by the state in the guise of the British Transport Commission, but the City Coach Company was not. In February 1952 the CCC sold out to the BTC, and was finally wound up in 1954. The CCC was well loved. With a service every fifteen minutes from north London to Southend via Romford, Brentwood and Billericay, its brown and cream buses offered strong competition to the railways – and its engineering standards were very high.

In September 1949, under the resumption of a pre-war plan, the line from Liverpool Street to Shenfield was electrified, and in September 1953 BR announced that electric trains would be extended to Chelmsford and Southend, to relieve pressure on the former London, Tilbury and Southend line, which was being rebuilt before it could be electrified. The *Billericay Times* headline for

No. 97 High Street was the library from 1950 until the current building was built. (Basildon Heritage)

Woolworths, 1950s. (Basildon Heritage)

2 October stated that electric trains would be running to Southend by 1957. Work commenced on the electrification of 13 miles of line in the summer of 1954, at a cost of £2.5m. The first electric train to pass through Billericay was on 30 November 1956, when a trial run was made to Rayleigh. On 11 December the first electric train reached Southend under its own power, and the new electric service came into operation on 31 December. An off-peak service of about one train an hour on Mondays to Saturdays was replaced by a service offering three trains an hour. The *Billericay Times* published a feature about the start of electric services, including a picture of one of the new trains and the complete timetable, as did the *Southend Standard*. BR even made a film about the electrification, entitled *Service to Southend*, and received glowing praise for having completed the job on time. While many rejoiced in the new clean electric trains, the passing of steam was seen as the end of an era by others. Steam locomotives did not disappear for some years, though: they still worked goods and parcels trains, and excursion trains from outside the electrified area, until their replacement by diesel engines or diesel railcars. It is believed that the last steam train through Billericay was on 29 August 1961, when a ballast train was hauled to and from the Southminster branch.

At the beginning of the 1960s Billericay station was redeveloped, with a rectangular extension being built along the north side of the ticket/parcels office to improve the handling of parcels. The side stairs to the platforms were rebuilt. On 5 June 1967 the station, along with the others on the line, ceased to handle goods traffic. The goods shed was demolished later, and the goods yard was turned into a car park.

Even before the electrification of the line was complete, it would appear from the evidence of season ticket sales that there was an influx of new residents not only into Billericay itself but also into its hinterland. According to Ken Butcher, tickets issued at the station rose from 6,400 in 1955 to 14,000 in 1957 and to 34,000 in 1962. That is a phenomenal growth. The electrification of the railway accelerated Billericay's development into a dormitory town for London. Much of the surrounding countryside was developed as part of this process, with the unfortunate effect of driving up property prices in the villages: most youngsters have had to move from village to town. Villages have become suburbs, with the unfortunate effect that the boundaries of what might be termed Greater Billericay do not correspond with the local authority boundaries. Places like Ramsden Heath and Stock, while part of Greater Billericay, are within the Chelmsford local authority boundary.

A train hauled by a Class B1 steam locomotive arrives at Billericay station, 1953. (David Collins)

Electrifying the railway at Billericay, 1955. (David Collins)

Everyday life continued through the 1950s, with few major events to ruffle what was still a relatively tranquil existence – despite Billericay's changing role in the world. On the night of 31 January/1 February 1953, however, disaster struck, with the great East Coast flood. This has been described as 'the worst natural disaster to befall Britain during the twentieth century', and affected a massive swathe of coastline from Yorkshire to Kent. Canvey Island was inundated, and Billericay was one of the places to which its residents were temporarily evacuated. Casualties were taken to Billericay Hospital.

National celebrations marked the coronation of Queen Elizabeth II on 2 June 1953. On the preceding Sunday there was a united service in Lake Meadows Park, attended by the Rev. S. Powley (Church of England), W. Purdy (Methodist) and J. Wilkinson (Congregational), as well as Sea Scouts and Cubs. The Billericay Brotherhood Band accompanied the singing. The plans for Coronation Day itself included a fancy dress parade, dancing and a bonfire, all in Lake Meadows Park, but heavy rain caused these plans to be amended. The fancy dress parade was held in the Archer Hall, and the other events were postponed until 13 June – the day of the town pageant.

As in any town, proposals of major change were often perceived as threatening long-established modes of existence. On 23 July 1954 a public meeting was held in Billericay to protest at the proposal by Walthamstow Borough Council (at that time in Metropolitan Essex, now part of Greater London) to build housing estates in Billericay. Over 1,000 people attended, with speeches being relayed to those assembled in the car park outside. MP Bernard Braine made the point that there was insufficient industry in the area to employ these potential new residents, and that the transport infrastructure was inadequate for them to work elsewhere. Billericay had its own problems without importing people from Metropolitan Essex. The meeting gave unanimous approval to a resolution that called on the Minister of Housing and Local Government to refuse to sanction the scheme, and to order an inquiry. Unfortunately the protest was to no avail, as Walthamstow Borough Council did indeed build houses at Billericay. The early 1950s also saw the building of the Town Farm estate (with the roads named after the 1953 Everest expedition) by Billericay UDC, and the continued development of South Green and the Chantry estate of the London Co-Operative Housing Society, which had started in the interwar years. All this meant that the population of the town rose from 6,949 in 1951 to 10,940 in 1961, and 17,246 in 1971.

Kitt's, which occupied 6 High Street from 1956. (Basildon Heritage)

Shelley's, 1950s. (Basildon Heritage)

In the late 1950s and early 1960s a young Billericay man named Wynford Grant came to national prominence. Wynford moved to Billericay at the age of ten in 1956, and aged twelve became the youngest ever newspaper editor, starting the *Billericay Observer* on 27 February 1958. Wynford was interviewed by Fyfe Robertson on the *Tonight* programme on BBC television in 1959 and by Alan Whicker on the same programme in 1961. The *Billericay Observer* lasted until December 1962, closing because Wynford had to study for his O levels! He wasn't finished, though – later producing a series of pamphlets on Billericay's history, including a short history of the town, writing the *Billericay Reference Book* and the *Billericay and District Quarterly Historical Review* – which only lasted for three editions. He also wrote a short history of Stock and several articles in the *Essex Countryside* magazine.

On the evening of 5 September 1958 there was an atrocious storm. In Wickford over 3in of rain fell in ninety minutes. Between 8 and 9pm a recorder at a meteorological station in Harrow recorded 1,470 lighting flashes within a radius of 10 to 15 miles, which was described as probably the most spectacular of the century. The storm affected Sussex, Kent and Essex, and eventually

Farrer's the undertakers is still with us. This view was photographed in the 1950s. (Basildon Heritage)

settled over Chelmsford. People were stranded in Billericay overnight, as many trains were cancelled. At the Ritz cinema water poured in through the front entrance and out through the lower exit. Flooding was more than 1ft deep in Orchard Avenue, considerable damage was done in Perry Street and several houses near the brook were flooded. For a time it was impossible for cars to reach Chelmsford, and some people in Wickford spent the night on the top deck of a bus. Stranded motorists were supplied with cups of tea. It took two days to clear up.

It was at the General Election in October 1959, when Edward (later Sir Edward) Gardiner was elected MP, that Billericay was the first constituency to declare its result, just fifty-seven minutes after the poll closed. The conservative Edward Gardiner held his seat in 1964, but lost in the 1966 election to Eric Moonman, Labour.

On 7 May 1960 the Cater Museum opened, founded by Alice Mary Cater (1900–62) as a memorial to her husband, William Alexander Cater (1870–1944). She aimed to establish a collection of bygones that preserved for all time some of Billericay's historical past; this was appropriate because William had been a Fellow of the Antiquarian Society. The search for premises started before the end of the Second World War. Mrs Cater expressed her ideas to the Billericay Local Group of the Council for the Protection of Rural England (the Billericay Society since 1972), which in 1944 published a booklet entitled *A Plan for Billericay*, which set out its views on the preservation and future development of the town. Harry Richman, also a member of the group, was recruited to co-ordinate what was to become the Billericay Collection of Bygones. In 1958 a site was found at 74 High Street, following the death of the house's occupant, Fred Eales. Alterations were made, and the museum was opened. The first curator was Harry Richman, author of *Billericay and its High Street*; he was succeeded in 1971 by Ted Wright, author of *Billericay Times*. Following Ted's death in 2000 he was succeeded by Christine Brewster.

In 1962 Billericay Residents' Association merged with Buttsbury Residents' Association to create the Billericay District Residents' Association. During the 1970s the Association held all nine Billericay seats on Basildon District Council.

On Boxing Day 1962 the snow started, and bad weather continued into March. It was said to be the worst winter since 1814. Basildon councillors complained that Billericay's roads received special snow clearance treatment, while in other places roads were left in chaos. A Labour member said that Billericay always got the best of everything, as that was where the money was.

B.U.D.C.
WARD 1
Billericay Coronation Celebrations Committee

Coronation Souvenir
Programme
June 1953

PRICE 1/-

Left The cover of Billericay's coronation souvenir, 1953. (Julia Seaman collection)

Below Billericay's coronation celebrations, 1953. (Julia Seaman collection)

FOR YOUR ENTERTAINMENT

May 30th.-June 8th SHOPPING WEEK Window Dressing and Word Competition. Particulars and entry forms from any Shopkeeper in High Street

Sunday May 31st. NATIONAL CHURCH SERVICE
Lake Meadows 3p.m.

Monday June 1st. CORONATION BALL (Archer Hall)

Tuesday June 2nd. CORONATION DAY

TELEVISION in Women's Institute Hall for Old Folk by kind co-operation of Mr. S. C. Squires. Tickets from Mr. Brooks

    6 p.m.   FANCY DRESS COMPETITION (Lake Meadows)

    7.30 p.m. SQUARE DANCE DEMONSTRATION by Bob Clayton (Lake Meadows)

    8-10p.m. DANCING ON THE LAWN (Lake Meadows)

    10 p.m. BONFIRE, FIRE WORKS (Lake Meadows)

Wednesday June 3rd OLD FOLKS TEA Archer Hall 3 p.m.

Thursday June 4th CHILDRENS TEA Gt. Burstead will assemble at senior School for display of Country Dancing then disperse to their respective schools for tea.

Friday June 5th Perry Street school to assemble at St. John's school at 2p.m.

Saturday June 6th OLDE TYME BALL (Archer Hall)

Sunday June 7th CONCERT (for the patients in St. Andrews)

Friday June 12th WOMENS HOCKEY MATCH
Lake Meadows 7 p.m. Past County Players v Present County Players

Saturday June 13th PAGEANT (Lake Meadows) See Back Page and separate Programme

FOR YOUR INFORMATION

June 1st-6th BILLERICAY CAMERA CLUB EXHIBITION
(Reading Rooms) 10.30 a.m. - 10p.m.

June 8th-13th FOUR CENTURIES EXHIBITION see Programme for further details. 2.30 - 9p.m. daily

CORONATION BEAKERS For under Five years old will be issued from the **Womens Institute Hall Billericay on MONDAY 1st (2-4p.m.) THURSDAY 4th (10 a.m. - noon) FRIDAY 5th (10 a.m. - noon) SATURDAY 6th 2-4p.m. of June.**

C.P.R.E. Particulars and details of a presentation to commemorate this occasion :-

OAK ROAD SIGN depicting "MAYFLOWER" appropriately coloured.
DESIGNED by the Chairman Mr. G. S. Amos A.I.A.A.
PRESENTED by the President Mrs. A. M. Cater.
EXECUTED by Messrs. H. & K. Mabbitt, Woodcarvists & Armorists, who have been responsible for much work in connection with churches all over Essex.
To be erected on the site of the Festival of Britain Tree planting corner Mountnessing Road and London Road.

OLDEST RESIDENTS Miss Emily Clark 98yrs. Mrs. Attridge 90yrs.
    Mrs. Clark 89yrs. Mrs. C. Reeve 88yrs.

OLDEST ESTABLISHED BUSINESS Bassoms (nearly 200 yrs.)
    Gentrys (about 150 yrs.)   Nix (about 145 yrs.)

OLDEST BUILDINGS Chantry Barn (rear of Chequers) Medieval
    Church Tower 1490   Red Lion 15th Century

Above Cramphorns at 148 High
Street, before its demolition. (Basildon
Heritage)

Right Cover of the Billericay Design
Statement. (Billericay Design
Statement Association)

Churchill Johnson's timber and builders' merchant, 1950s. (Basildon Heritage)

No. 99 High Street was Groves the outfitters. (Basildon Heritage)

Harringtons, *c.*1960, a few years before its closure and demolition. (Basildon Heritage)

Council officials said that this was not true; it was just that Billericay had the hospital.

In 1966 Tilbury and South East Essex Hospital Management Committee, of which St Andrew's Hospital was a part, became the South Essex Hospital Management Committee. During the post-war years St Andrew's flourished, but in the early 1970s it was decided to open a new hospital at Basildon. In 1973, when the new hospital opened, St Andrew's became a regional plastic surgery and rehabilitation unit. This became internationally renowned, but in 1998 the unit was moved to Broomfield Hospital in Chelmsford, and most of the old hospital was redeveloped into housing. Some of the old workhouse buildings were listed.

The Times of 22 July 1969 included a frivolous article, written in connection with the launch from Cape Kennedy of the Apollo 11 astronauts for the first moon landing. It was reported that while Neil Armstrong, Buzz Aldrin and Michael Collins were blasting off to the moon, in the House of Commons in London there was a moon man speaking: he was Eric Moonman, the Labour MP for Billericay.

From the mid-1960s until the 1990s there were a number of disputes on the railway. One form of industrial action employed by the drivers' unions was an overtime and rest day working ban, along with working to rule. During one

The Cater Museum occupies an eighteenth-century building. (Author)

Below, from left

The title page of *Billericay and its High Street*. (Billericay Society)

A Plan for Billericay. (Julia Seaman collection/ Billericay Society)

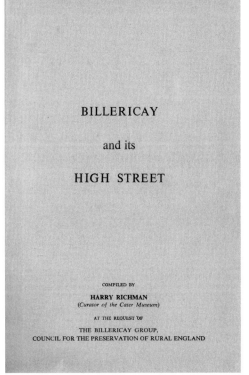

BILLERICAY

and its

HIGH STREET

COMPILED BY
HARRY RICHMAN
(Curator of the Cater Museum)

AT THE REQUEST OF

THE BILLERICAY GROUP,
COUNCIL FOR THE PRESERVATION OF RURAL ENGLAND

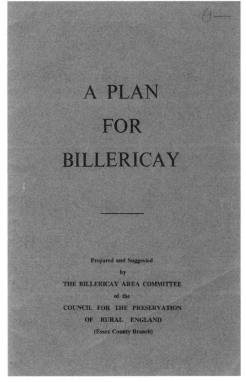

A PLAN

FOR

BILLERICAY

Prepared and Suggested
by
THE BILLERICAY AREA COMMITTEE
of the
COUNCIL FOR THE PRESERVATION
OF RURAL ENGLAND
(Essex County Branch)

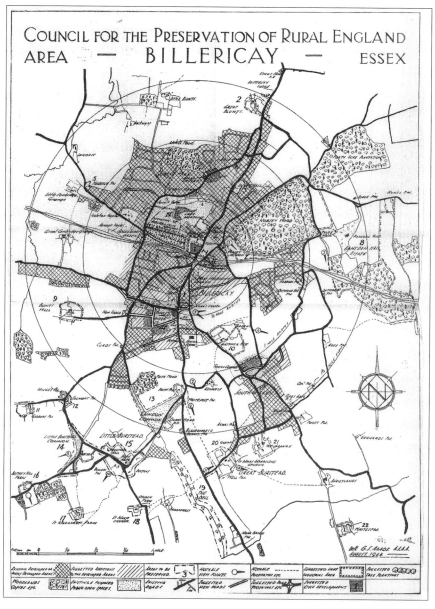

The map from *A Plan for Billericay*. (Julia Seaman collection/Billericay Society)

dispute, on 7 January 1974, the police had to be called to Billericay station when some commuters, desperate to get on to an already overcrowded train, forced their way into an empty driver's cab and the guard's van, and refused to leave.

In 1972 the Congregational church celebrated the tercentenary of its official founding by publishing a history, *Calling the Generations*. That same year it joined the newly formed United Reform Church – a union of Congregationalists and English Presbyterians. Also in church news, in 1977 the Billericay and Little Burstead Team Ministry was created. This initially comprised Christ Church (built in Perry Street in 1963), St Mary the Virgin at Little Burstead and St Mary Magdalen, with St John the Divine at Outwood Common (dedicated in 1968) being added in 1991. By the mid-1970s St Mary Magdalen was proving to be too small. After fifteen years of praying, planning and fundraising, the Archer Hall in Laindon Road was demolished, and a new church – the Emmanuel church – was built on the site, opening on 14 June 1992. This at last fulfilled the wish of the late Miss Georgina Archer, and Emmanuel took over as the town's main church. St Mary Magdalen was refurbished for use as an ecumenical centre in 2007.

Billericay was continuing to grow. In the 1970s it was decided to build approximately 1,500 homes and supporting infrastructure at Queen's Park. Plans stalled when many of the owners of the plots of land here could not be traced, and eventually the whole area was compulsorily purchased by Moody Homes. Despite the increasing population, fashions in entertainment were changing, and in the face of competition from television the Ritz cinema closed its doors for the last time in 1971. Bingo followed, and when this fell out of fashion in the mid-1980s the building was converted to a snooker hall and renamed the Radion Snooker Club. This did not save the building, however, and despite attempts to have the building listed and objections by Billericay Town Council it was demolished in 2001 – and replaced by rather unattractive flats.

Since its foundation in 1880, Billericay Town Football Club had been very successful, progressing through the Mid-Essex League, the Southern Essex Combination and the Essex Olympian League, before in 1971 becoming founder members of the Essex Senior League and in 1977 the Athenian League. They became champions in 1978/9, and after two seasons were elected to the Isthmian League. In 1976 the club won the FA Vase at Wembley beating Stamford in extra time, and in 1977 they went to Wembley again,

Emmanuel church, built in the 1990s to replace Archer Hall. (Author)

High Street and Barnsley House, 1970s. (Basildon Heritage)

Bush Hall Stores parade. (Author)

Queen's Park, before redevelopment in the 1970s. (Basildon Heritage)

Queen's Park, with the new development under construction. (Basildon Heritage)

drawing with Sheffield FC but beating them in the replay. The *Recorder* the week before the match included a special supplement on the team, and the Sunday afterwards people lined the streets to pay tribute to the manager John Newman and his team. In 1979 Billericay were back at Wembley, winning the FA Vase for the third time when they beat Almondsbury Greenway. Doug Young's hat trick was the first at Wembley since Geoff Hurst's in the 1966 World Cup Final. Billericay were the first team to win the FA Vase three times. Billericay Town eventually progressed to the Isthmian League Premier Division, and at the end of the 2011–12 season was promoted to the Football Conference South Division.

In 1976 Norsey Wood was acquired by Basildon District (now Borough) Council, who provide a warden and an information centre, near the car park off Outwood Common Road. There is a large map nearby, and information about the wood can be found on the website of the Norsey Wood Society, founded in 1977.

On Saturday 4 June 1977 the Silver Jubilee of Queen Elizabeth II was celebrated with a procession in the High Street, which started at 1.30pm and wound through the streets to the Mayflower Hospital League of Friends fete at the Sun Corner. Five thousand people packed the High Street. The procession was led by the Silver Jubilee princess, seventeen-year-old Jane Hatch, who opened the fete. The event made a profit of £2,000. In the following week there was a gala dance organised by the Chamber of Trade, while at Great Burstead on Tuesday 7 June 750 people watched a sedan chair race between twenty-four teams. Few completed the course. Afterwards there was a giant picnic in the church grounds, followed by a pillow-fight joust by members of the parish. After a short church service there was a disco.

In the General Election of 1970 Robert McCrindle took Billericay back for the Conservatives. From 1974 Billericay was part of the new Basildon constituency, but in 1983 the town regained its own constituency. The new MP was the former Basildon MP, Harvey Proctor. While he was a good constituency MP, he was controversial in his views on immigration: he thought the number of 'coloured' immigrants should be restricted, and that paid repatriation should be introduced; he also favoured capital punishment. In 1986 he was involved in a scandal involving under-age male prostitutes, but despite this, and further allegations, he won the backing of his constituency association. In the spring of 1987 he was charged with gross indecency and resigned his candidature. In a rather different contribution to the rich tapestry of Billericay's history, this colourful character compiled (with Vic Meacham) a book of old postcards of the town and surrounding area. Harvey Proctor was succeeded by Teresa Gorman, who was and is something of a colourful character. She was one of the rebels over the Maastricht Treaty, who nearly brought down John Major's government. She held the seat in the 1992 and 1997 elections, and in 2001 was succeeded by John Baron in 2001; he held the seat for the Conservatives in 2005, and in 2010 he won the new constituency of Basildon and Billericay.

It was Billericay's turn for some more extreme weather. On the night of 15/16 October 1987 there was a hurricane. Mature trees were uprooted as if they were mere saplings, telegraph poles were torn up, roads were blocked with fallen trees, power cables were brought down. Teams of people got together to clear roads and paths, but for a time there were no trains or buses. People couldn't get to work and schools were closed. The Stock Road (Billericay end) saw the most damage, being blocked for most of the day. Near Barleylands Farm an articulated lorry was blown off the road, and the driver and his passenger had to be cut from the cab. It is estimated that Norsey Wood lost 5,000 trees, with some of the most historic trees falling victim to the wind. Some of these

Norsey Wood visitor centre. (Author)

The entrance to Norsey Wood. (Author)

The 1960 replacement for North Sea House. (Basildon Heritage)

The health centre, Stock Road. (Basildon Heritage)

Above A 1970s shop development in the High Street. (Basildon Heritage)

Right Billericay is twinned with two American towns, Billerica, Massachusetts, and Fishers, Indiana, as well as Chauvigny, France. (Author)

were up to 300 years old and included a 300-year-old horse chestnut that was reputed to have been used as the town gallows. On 25 January 1990 there was another hurricane, this time during the day. Trees were uprooted, roofs were ripped off and bus shelters were toppled. Trains couldn't run through Billericay, and British Rail organised a fleet of buses from Shenfield through Billericay to Wickford.

In 1995, to commemorate the fiftieth anniversary of VE Day, the May Day Bank Holiday Monday was postponed from the 1st to the 8th, the actual anniversary. Townspeople filled St Mary Magdalen for a service led by the Rev. Peter Ashton, preceded by wreath-laying at the war memorial.

Under the Local Government Reorganisation of 1974 Basildon UDC became Basildon District Council. Following the Local Government Commission for England's review of all local authorities, in 1992 a group of Billericay people formed a steering committee to campaign for parish councils

Lake Meadows. (Author)

in the area. In 1997 the new parishes of Billericay, Great Burstead and South Green, Little Burstead, Ramsden Crays and Ramsden Bellhouse were created. The Town Council offices are in Crown Yard. In October 2010 Basildon District Council had borough status confirmed on it by the queen, and became Basildon Borough Council.

On 31 December 1999 hundreds of townspeople filled the High Street for a special candlelight procession down to the Sun Corner to celebrate the second millennium. Choirs kept the party spirit alight by singing through the evening, and the night was topped off with a bumper firework display. Similar jollification occurred to mark the Golden Jubilee of Queen Elizabeth II in 2002, when there was an all day celebration in Lake Meadows on Saturday 1 June. This featured Abba, Rod Stewart and Tina Turner tribute acts and a spectacular firework finale. Roads throughout the town were shut off for traditional street parties. Celebrations continued in 2010, to mark the centenary of the Catholic parish of the Holy Redeemer. These included a mass on 13 September, led by the Bishop of Brentwood. The fiftieth anniversary of the Cater Museum was on 7 May in the same year, but as the 7th was a Friday the celebrations were transferred to the 8th. On 29 April 2011, to mark the wedding of Prince William to Catherine Middleton, street parties were held in many parts of the town.

The High Street continued to change, with some developments being more positive than others. On 2 January 2009 Woolworths closed – to be replaced by Iceland at the end of May. Swan Books shut at the end of April, and the popular local music shop Slipped Discs (described online as 'the most comfortable record shop on the planet') moved up the High Street into the vacated premises. There was more good news in mid-March 2012, when WHSmith opened in the High Street – so the town has a bookseller once again. During the latter half of 2011 and the beginning of 2012 Billericay station was redeveloped, with the addition of a new ticket hall – meaning that the extension built in the early 1960s for parcels traffic had to be demolished.

The lake at Lake Meadows, 2010. (Author)

The modern Billericay library. (Author)

Offices adjacent to the railway station. (Basildon Heritage)

The Baptist church in Chapel Street. (Author)

Iceland, which has taken over the Woolworths premises. (Author)

The High Street, early 2008. (Author)

Chapel Street, early 2008. (Author)

The Blue Boar takes its name from an old Billericay tavern. (Author)

Billericay has, in a manner of speaking, featured in television comedy. Three series of the BBC's *Gavin and Stacey* were transmitted between 2007 and 2010. The programmes were largely filmed in Cardiff, Barry and the surrounding area, and very little (if any) in Billericay – parts of Cardiff standing in for the town.

In 2010 the Billericay Community Archive Group was formed. This is run in partnership with Essex County Council Libraries and the Essex Record Office, and is funded by a grant from the Heritage Lottery Fund – but it is run by the people of Billericay. It has its own website, www.billericayhistory.org.uk, and comes under the umbrella of Basildon Borough Heritage and Museum Group.

It seems fitting to conclude this book with the celebrations on 2 to 5 June 2012 that marked the sixtieth anniversary of the accession of Queen Elizabeth II. In Billericay as elsewhere, the main celebrations took place on Monday the 4th. The streets were lined with bunting and flags as residents laid on street parties. While the weather had been bright and sunny, at the weekend it had turned rather wet – but fortunately on the 4th the rain held off. The culmination of the celebrations was the lighting of a beacon at Sun Corner at 10.15pm, to great cheers from the flag-waving crowd. The national anthem was then belted out by those on Sun Corner and by scores of people lining the street, and the

The fire station, built in the 1970s. (Author)

Waitrose is a fairly new building, dating from 1999.(Author)

party continued late into the night in the High Street's pubs. Longer-lasting symbols of the Jubilee are to be the only Queen Elizabeth II playing field in Essex owned by the county council, and a new Jubilee Wood. The playing field has come about because, after five years of trying, in August 2012 the Town Council finally secured the 15-acre green space at Sun Corner, which had been left to the people of Billericay by a farmer in the 1930s. Having fallen under the aegis of the County Council, its maintenance had been in the hands of Basildon Borough Council and its predecessors, but there had never been any formal proposal for its development. The Jubilee Wood, also at Sun Corner, is being created initially with 100 oak saplings, provided by the Woodland Trust.

Who knows what is in store for Billericay? Speaking personally, I feel that the town deserves to become a separate authority, with those parts of its hinterland in the Basildon Borough and Chelmsford City areas incorporated into it. I urge the people of Billericay to remember their heritage and regain their independence. Remember 1381 – but this time don't be defeated!

Harry Richman (1911–71) came to Billericay in the early 1930s and immediately developed an instant and deep affection for the town. Anthony Nicholl, the town's first local historian, was instrumental in inspiring Harry to understand Billericay.

From the early 1930s until the early 1950s Harry spent much of his leisure time walking round the town and surrounding villages with a pencil and a notebook in hand, sketching anything that caught his eye. These rough drawings were later turned into pen and ink sketches, and some of these later became watercolours. Harry was an accomplished painter, and recorded many of the town's buildings as well as some in the surrounding villages. He acquired this artistic talent from his father.

Harry was also an accomplished modelmaker; he made a large model of the High Street and Chapel Street, together with other historic buildings. This was exhibited at a Festival of Britain exhibition in the Mayflower Hall in 1951, and, while normally stored in the Cater Museum, has also been exhibited elsewhere, for example in the Reading Rooms in September 2010.

Harry's absorption in the history and folklore of Billericay led him in 1953 to produce the first edition of his *Billericay and its High Street*. A second and expanded edition with a supplement followed in 1963. This book, which also covers the railway station and what were St Andrew's Hospital and Chapel, is the definitive work on the area – the best book on Billericay's history.

When Alice Cater decided to set up the Cater Museum, Harry gave her much practical advice on its layout. He was appointed its first curator: a very appropriate choice.

Harry died in 1971. A book of his and his father's paintings and sketches of Billericay and the surrounding area was published by the Cater Museum to mark its fiftieth anniversary in May 2010.

BIBLIOGRAPHY AND SOURCES

Addison, William, *Essex Heyday* (Dent, 1949)

Amos, G., *A History and Description of the Parish Church of St Mary Magdalen* (The Parish of St Mary Magdalen, 1959)

Austen, Frederick, *The Rectors of Two Essex Parishes and Their Times* (Benham, 1943)

Austin, Geoff, *Another Miller's tale – the history of Mountnessing* (Mountnessing Parish Council, 1994)

Baedeker, *Baedeker's Guide to Great Britain* (Baedeker, 1937)

Baedeker, *Baedeker's Guide to Great Britain, Volume 1* (Baedeker, 1966)

Booker, John, *Essex and the Industrial Revolution* (Essex County Council, 1974)

Billericay Archaeological and Historical Society, *Billericay in 1900* (Billericay Archaeological and Historical Society, 1999)

Boyer, Paul S., Clark, Clifford Edward Jr, Kett, Joseph F., Salisbury, Neal, Sitkoff, Harvard, Woloch, Nancy, *The Enduring Vision* (Houghton Mifflin, 2002)

Boyes, John and Russell, David, *The Canals of Eastern England* (David and Charles, 1977)

Brown, Arthur, *Essex at Work 1700–1815* (Essex County Council, 1969)

Brown, Arthur, *Meagre Harvest* (Essex Record Office, 1990)

Brown, Arthur, *Prosperity and Poverty – Rural Essex 1700–1815* (Essex Record Office, 1996)

Carpenter, Roger, *Christopher Martin, Great Burstead and the Mayflower* (Barstable, 1982)

Carpenter, Roger, *An Index to Billericay and its High Street (by Harry Richman)* (Barstable, 1993)

Carson, Patricia, *The Fair Face of Flanders* (Ianoo, 1991)

Cook, K.G., *The History of Norsey Wood* (Basildon District Council, 1984)

Clark, Andrew, Munson, James, Briggs, Asa (eds), *Echoes of the Great War: the diary of the Reverend Andrew Clark 1914–1919* (Oxford University Press, 1985)

Crawley, R.J., MacGregor, D.R.and Simpson, F.D., *The Years Between, Volume 1* (MacGregor, 1979)

Crawley, R.J., MacGregor, D.R.,and Simpson, F.D., *The Years Between, Volume 2* (Oxford, 1984)

Dicks, Sheridan, *Buttsbury Recollections of the 20th Century* (Sheridan Dicks, 2001)

Doyle, Paul A., *Fields of the First* (Forward Airfield Research, 1997)

Edwards, A.C., *John Petre* (Regency Press, 1975)

Edwards, A.C., *A History of Essex* (Phillimore, 2000)

Emmison, F.G., and Lynham, E., *Catalogue of Maps in the Essex Record Office 1566–1855* (Essex County Council, 1947)

Emmison, F.G., *Tudor Secretary* (Longmans Green, 1961).

Emmison, F.G., *Tudor Food and Pastimes* (Benn, 1964)

Emmison, F.G., *Guide to the Essex Record Office* (Essex County Council, 1969)

Emmison, F.G., *Elizabethan Life: Disorder* (Essex Record Office, 1970)

Emmison, F.G., *Elizabethan Life: Morals and the Church Courts* (Essex Record Office, 1973)

Emmison, F.G., *Elizabethan Life: Home, Work and Land* (Essex Record Office, 1976)

Emmison, F.G., *Elizabethan Life: Essex Gentry's Wills* (Essex Record Office, 1978)

Emmison, F.G., *Elizabethan Life: Wills of Essex Gentry and Yeoman* (Essex Record Office, 1980)

Farries, Kenneth G., *Essex Windmills, Millers and Millwrights, Volume 1, An Historical Review* (Skilton, 1981)

Farries, Kenneth G., *Essex Windmills, Millers and Millwrights Volume 2, A Technical Review* (Skilton, 1982)

Farries, Kenneth G., *Essex Windmills, Millers and Millwrights Volume 3, A Review by Parishes A–E* (Skilton, 1984)

Foster, Stewart, *The Catholic Church in Stock* (McMahon, 1991)

Friar, Stephen, *The Sutton Companion to Local History* (Sutton, 2004)

Grant, Wynford, *Early Billericay* (Grant, 1962)

Grant, Wynford, *The Mills of Billericay* (Grant, 1962)

Grant, Wynford, *Billericay and the Mayflower and the Place Names of Billericay* (Grant, 1962)

Grant, Wynford, *The Inns of Billericay* (Grant, 1963)

Grant, Wynford, *A Short History of Billericay* (Grant, 1965)

Green, Roger, *Billericay – An Historical Tour in Pictures* (Phillimore,1997)

Green, Roger, *Billericay – A Pictorial History* (Phillimore, 2005)

Harper, William, *Billericay Through the Ages* (Chanticleer, 1969)

Jackson, Queenie, *St Andrew's Hospital* (Perivan Colour Print, 1983)

Jarvis, L. Donald, *Stock, Essex* (Bevan, 1934)

Jarvis, L. Donald, *With Respect* (Stock Parish Council, 1995)

Kay, Peter, *The London, Tilbury and Southend Railway, Volume 1* (Kay, 1996)

Kay, Peter, *The London, Tilbury and Southend Railway, Volume 2* (Kay, 1997)

Kay, Peter, *The London, Tilbury and Southend Railway, Volume 3* (Kay, 2010)

Kemble, James, *Prehistoric and Roman Essex* (Tempus, 2001)

Kent, Sylvia, *Billericay Voices* (Tempus, 2002)

Kent, Sylvia, *The Billericay School* (Tempus, 2003)

Kent, Sylvia, *St Mary Magdalen – The Church in the High Street* (The Parish, 2007)

Liddell, W.H. and Wood, R.G.E. (eds), *Essex and the Great Revolt* (Essex Record Office, 1982)

MacFarlane, Alan, *Witchcraft in Tudor and Stuart England* (Routledge & Kegan Paul, 1970)

Morant, Philip, *History and Antiquities of the County of Essex* (Osborne, 1768)

Neale, Kenneth, *Essex in History* (Phillimore, 1997)

Nix, William, *The Catholic Church in Billericay* (Holy Redeemer Catholic Church, c.1987)

Osborne, Alan, *City Fact File* (Essex Bus Enthusiast Group, 2002)

Osborne, Alan and Young, J.R., *Westcliff-on-Sea Motor Services Ltd. An Outline History* (Farley, 2011)

Phillips, Charles, *The Shenfield to Southend Line* (Oakwood, 1984)

Phillips, Charles, *The Story of Stock and Buttsbury* (Ian Henry, 2002)

Proctor, K. Harvey and Meecham, Vic, *Billericay in Old Picture Postcards* (European Library, 1985)

Richardson, John, *The Local Historian's Encyclopedia* (Historical Publications, 2003)

Richman, Harry, *Billericay and its High Street* (Billericay Group Council for the Preservation of Rural England, 1963.)

Roche, Aloysius, *The Catholic Church, Billericay* (Youngman, c.1963)

Rusiecki, Paul, *The Impact of Catastrophe – The People of Essex and the First World War 1914–1920* (Essex Record Office, 2008)

Rumble, Alexander (ed.), *Domesday Book – Essex* (Phillimore, 1983)

Scollan, Maureen, *Sworn to Serve: Police in Essex 1840–1990* (Phillimore, 1993)

Smith, Ken, *Essex Under Arms: The Early Years to 1900* (Ian Henry, 1998)

Snell, Peter, *City Coach Company* (Essex Bus Enthusiasts Group, 1991)

Swindale, Dennis, *Branch Lines to Maldon* (East Anglian Railway Museum Publications, 2007)

Swindale, Dennis, *Branch Line to Southminster* (East Anglian Railway Museum Publications, 2008)

Tate, W.E., *The Parish Chest* (Phillimore, 1983)

Taylor, William, *Calling The Generations* (Billericay United Reform Church, 1972)

Walker, George, *The Story of a Little Town* (J.H. Clarke and Co., 1947)

Waywell, Robin and Jux, Frank, *Industrial Railways and Locomotives of Essex* (Industrial Railway Society, 2011)

Wright, Ted, *The Fate of the Zeppelin L32* (Chanticleer Publications, 1977)

Wright, Ted, *Billericay Times* (Cater Museum Trust, 1999)

Worcester, Robert, *A History and Guide to the Church of St Mary Magdalene, Great Burstead* (St Mary Magdalene Parish Church, Great Burstead, 1999)

Billericay and District Quarterly Historical Review (Grant, 1963)

Billericay and Wickford Standard Recorder, 1971 to 1973

Billericay Design Statement (Billericay Design Statement Association, 2010)

Billericay Times, 1931–65

Billericay Gazette 1979–2012

Billericay Standard Recorder, 1967–71

Billericay Standard Recorder, 1981–6

The Blairmore Enterprise, 1926

Bradshaw's Railway Guide 1889–1961 (Henry Blacklock and Company)

Billericay Gazette 1926 (HMSO, 1926)

Bus timetables for 1917–2007: National Steam Car Company, National Omnibus and Travel Company, Eastern National Omnibus Company, Westcliff-on-Sea Motor Services Ltd, City Coach Company, First Essex

Daily Mail, 1896–1996

Essex Archaeological Society Transactions, 1858–1926

Essex Chronicle, 1883–1957

Essex Review, 1892–1957 (Benham)

Essex Weekly News, 1883–1957

Evening Echo, 1969–2002

Great Eastern Journal, 1974–2012 (Great Eastern Railway Society)

Great Eastern Railway Public Timetables, 1889–1922

The Guardian and Observer Archive, 1791–2003

Kelly's Post Office Directory, 1845–1937

LNER Magazine, 1927–47

National Library of New Zealand Newspaper Collection, 1839–1945

The New York Times, 1851–1926

Pigot's Directory, 1822–3, 1832–3 and 1839

Railways South East, 1987–94 (Capital Transport Publishing)

Recorder, Billericay and Wickford edition, 1977–8

Southend Standard, 1889 to 1979

Standard Recorder, Billericay and Wickford edition, 1974 to 1975

The Times Archive, 1785–2006

Trove – Digitalised Newspapers, 1803–1954 (National Library of Australia)

The Universal British Directory, 1791

Billericay History

www.billericayhistory.org.uk

part of the South East Essex Community Archive Network

Billericayhistory.org.uk is home of the Billericay Community Archive – a repository of history, memories, photos, videos and opinions about Billericay and surrounding villages.

The Billericay Community Archive group was formed in 2010 in partnership with Essex County Council Libraries and the Essex Record Office, and funded by a grant from the Heritage Lottery Fund. It is run by the people of Billericay.

The Billericay Community Archive takes the form of an internet site, so that its content can be accessed from home computers, the People's Network in libraries around the county, and from a computer anywhere in the world.

The Community Archive gathers memories as well as copying photographs and other documents that relate to the history of the area. Billericay residents are asked to share their memories and photographs of life in the town and the surrounding areas.

The library is a drop-off point for your memories.

Do you need any help with the material you're thinking of adding to the website? Do you need help with writing your story, or help with publishing it to the site? Please email the editor with any questions at all: editor@billericayhistory.org.uk.